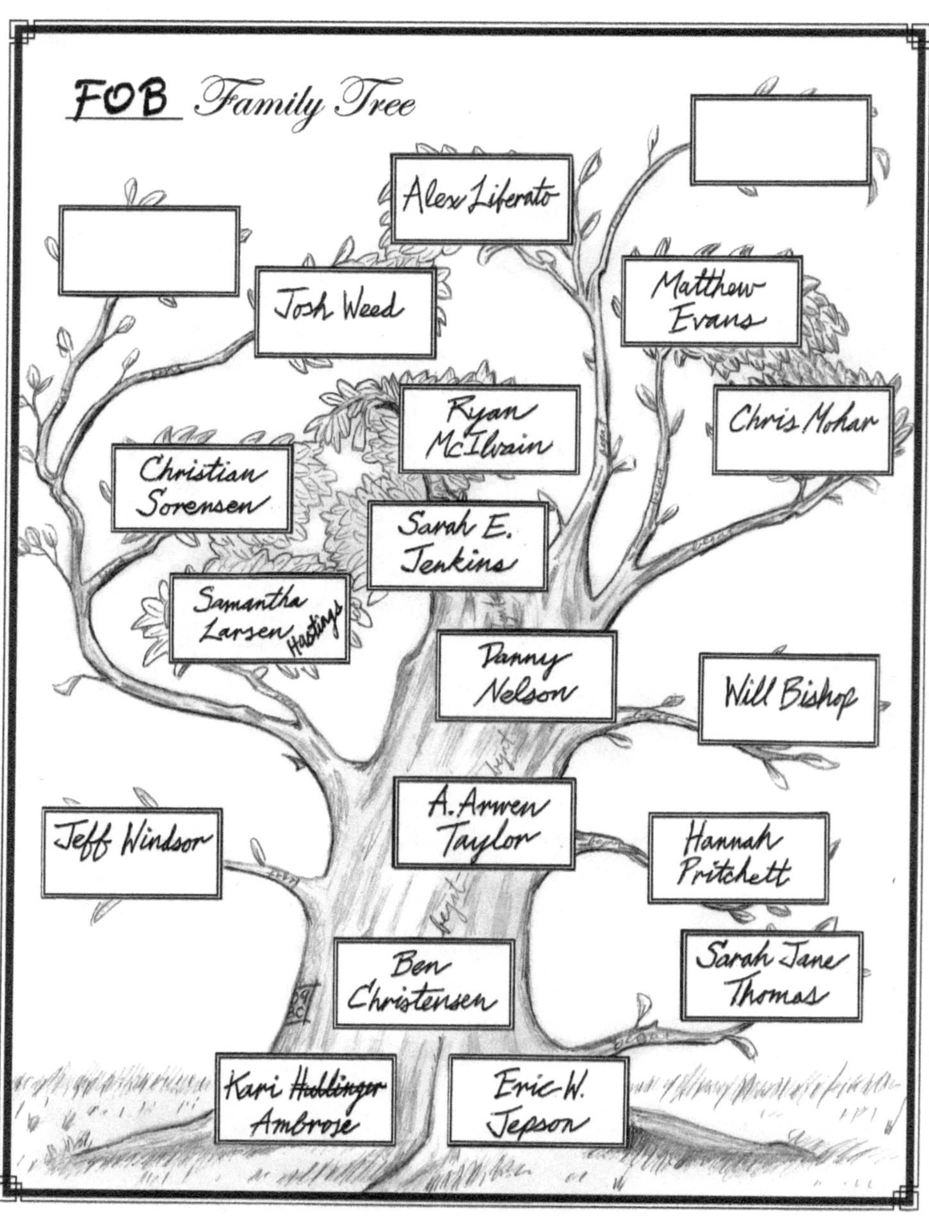
FOB Family Tree
Alex Liberato
Josh Weed
Matthew Evans
Ryan McIlvain
Chris Mohar
Christian Sorensen
Sarah E. Jenkins
Samantha Larsen Hastings
Danny Nelson
Will Bishop
Jeff Windsor
A. Arwen Taylor
Hannah Pritchett
Ben Christensen
Sarah Jane Thomas
Kari Hoblinger Ambrose
Eric W. Jepson

A QUOTIDIAN BOOK OF SCRIPTURE

CONTAINING, BUT NOT LIMITED TO, THE JUICIEST PORTIONS OF THE

OLD TESTAMENT

—sans, for obvious reasons, Judges 19—

translated through means of memory and nightmare
out of the pre-translated tongues (being mainly English):
and with the former translations ignored,

or—in special cases—
dictated but not read,

by His Fobbiness's
special command, in perpetuity,

worlds with very definite (and sometimes good-looking) ends,
albeit of a feminist bent in places,
with far too many references to behemoths and leviathans,
and thus, being indebted to the grace of your most gracious progenitrix,
published in the year of the FOB seven
(using the Jepsonian calendar for its ease of dates).

Fully Authorized Fob Version

Eric W Jepson

B.G. Christensen Sarah E. Jenkins Danny Nelson
editors

Peculiar Pages

AN IMPRINT OF B10 MEDIAWORX
KANSAS CITY MO

PUBLISHED BY

Peculiar Pages
115 Ramona Avenue
El Cerrito, CA 94530
peculiarpages.com

an imprint of
B10 Mediaworx
9754 N Ash Avenue, #204
Kansas City, MO 64157
b10mediaworx.com

The Fob Bible
Copyright © 2009 by Eric W Jepson, Danny Nelson, Arwen Taylor, Samantha Larsen Hastings,
         B.G. Christensen, Sarah Jenkins, Ryan McIlvains, William C. Bishop

Edited by: Eric W Jepson, B.G. Christensen, Sarah E. Jenkins, Danny Nelson

Illustrations: Paul Gustave Doré (1832-1883)

Book design: Elizabeth Beeton

Cover design: Lisa Yip and Xue Xue He of TechFutures, techfutures.org

All rights reserved

ISBN-13: 978-0-9817696-8-4
ISBN-10: 0-9817696-8-3

"How to Get Over It" is an excerpt from *Byuck: A Novel* by Eric W Jepson.

The Official History of the Society for the Spiritual Attunement of the Friends of G.C. Benefield, Chapter 34, is a complementary piece to the forthcoming *Freerider and Boost* series of novels by B.G. Christensen.

Publisher's Cataloging-In-Publication Data
(Prepared by The Donohue Group, Inc.)

The Fob bible : a quotidian book of scripture containing, but not limited to,
  the juiciest portions of the Old Testament / Eric W Jepson ... [et al.],
  editors ; illustrations: Paul Gustave Doré. -- Fully authorized Fob version

  p. : ill. ; cm.

  ISBN-13: 978-0-9817696-8-4
  ISBN-10: 0-9817696-8-3

  1. Bible. O.T.--Humor. 2. Bible--Parodies, imitations, etc. I. Jepson, Eric W. II. Doré, Gustave,
1832-1883.

PN6231.B45 F63 2009
817.6   2009902513

No matter where we stand today regarding our past,
we share a like hope for a gentler future.

Thus, in recognition of services to the future
greater than any served by our humble book,
proceeds from the sale of this volume are surrendered to
LDS Humanitarian Services
that they may build wells and vaccinate children
and otherwise better our troubled world.

Deuteronomy 15:8

Table of Contents

The opening of the King James Bible is simple yet supernal: "In the beginning God created the heaven and the earth." There is an understatement in the phrase that approaches transcendence, and one wonders if the transcribist of the tale isn't being slightly self-referential to his own translation when he concludes: "And God saw that it was good."

It is the genius of the Bible that it is a story which provides its own frame and its own apology; all the resultant confusion and chaos of the ages is simply the process by which we mortals return to the sublime simplicity of that opening statement: the procreant urge of creation, the Edenic peace of a world without contradiction. Should humanity fit the terms of one divine prearrangement, so the story goes, then that moment of creational joy can once more touch our tired telestial lives.

Little wonder that, ever since, mankind has earnestly tried to recast that moment of creation into something a little more palatable to those of us left alone with the million inconsistencies of our mortal struggle. Thus, we have the Lilith mythologies of the middle ages, the awkward but beautifully worded epics of Milton, the scientific explanation of a "mitochondrial Eve"—each an example of humanity trying to include ourselves in a narrative that minimizes the uncertainty of our experience.

Fob begins its history in Utah Valley, 2002, when chance meetings in college courses and writers conferences prompted Fob founders Kari Ambrose (then Hullinger), Ben Christensen, and Eric W Jepson (the W silent even then) to set up a regular writing group to discuss their writings and ambitions. As the first meeting was arranged by Ben Christensen, they eventually came to call themselves the Friends of Ben (providing an acronym that, considering the alternatives, was probably the best available at that time). From there, the group grew—perhaps even metastasized—bringing in poets, artists, linguists, and scientists, and garnering a small but dedicated fellowship. Today, members of Fob are located across the United States and England, and continue to meet to share ideas and writing across a wide range of genres and perspectives.

It is not puzzling, given the Mormon heritage of the group, that they would have an urge to reexamine fundamental assertions of their culture—some from positions of orthodoxy and others from points far removed. Fob from the beginning was a meeting of misfits, a place for those who felt somehow outside the day-to-day realities of modern pragmatics. Often, members of Fob might turn to the poetry of the Bible or other scriptural works as they worked out their own understanding of how they fit into a larger spectrum. As is inevitable among talented individuals, these examinations often flowered into creative works.

This book is the result of these examinations, and the fruit of those creative works. And—though we do say so ourselves—we see that it is good.

THE EDITORS
March 25, 2009

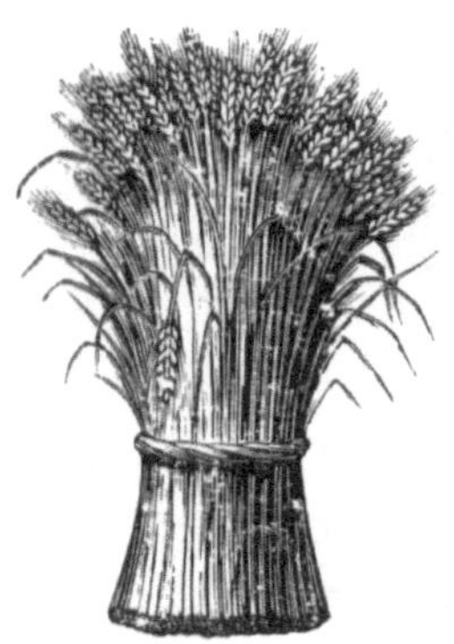

Acknowledgments

The Fob Collective, in addition to incestuously thanking each other, would like to acknowledge the assistance of:

Elizabeth Beeton

Anna Bennion

Lynsey Brasfield

Bryan Catanzaro

Jessie Christensen

Kyle Jepson

Lynsey Jepson

Moriah Jovan

the Malmrose family

Bill Murray

Heather Nelson

Regina Spektor

Aaron Thomas

your mom

And, particularly, the efforts of Kjerste Christensen, without whom this whole thing probably wouldn't have happened. Sorry for not calling you on the phone to say thanks, Kjerste, but frankly we have no idea how to pronounce your name.

THE SUN'S TEN FINGERS CAME UNFURLED.

In the beginning God created the heaven and the earth. And the earth was without form, and void; and darkness was upon the face of the deep.

Creation

The sun's ten fingers came unfurled.
He gathered struts and made a world.
With careful breath the sphere was blown:
a hollow ball of molten stone.
And with the glass-sharp stars in thrall,
he spun the geodesic ball.

The moon stretched out her oyster hand
and on the struts she lifted land.
In mercury streams the valleys bled:
the mountain shook its hoary head.
She set the rain in silver sheets
upon the ocean's stormy streets.

The sun shook out his golden beard
and with its heat the land was seared.
The gold-gray ash, 'neath greening rain,
bristled up in heads of grain.
The trees grew up at his approach,
and closed their gowns with emerald brooch.

The moon unbound her swelling womb
and scattered the world with ruby bloom.
She shrouded its eyes with birds in flight
and veiled its face with silky night.
Then balanced the sphere on a silver scale
and lined the seas with fishes' mail.

Then the sun and the moon
set the world in a swoon
and clothed it in meadow and wood.

And with bashful glance
began to dance

. . . and called it good.

PERHAPS HE IS MY ADAM.

I Study Barnett Newman's *Adam* (1951)

Maybe it's not
the first man, this block
of thick, choppy vertical
lines in dark red, darker purple.

Maybe it's his great
great great great grandson,
seen from the ribcage
out.

Maybe it's five
different Adams,
all posing in profile,
all paused in agony,
arms blood heavy
fingertips purpled
holding their breath, their muscles,
until the painting is complete.

Perhaps he is my Adam.

Maybe he is preparing
to bend his head
to whisper,

maybe
to stretch his hand out
to spark.

. . . SWITCHING THE STARS ON / LINE BY LINE.

Genesis

She formed beneath me
on a blanket
on the wet ground pushing
its wetness through—
the dew risen up on the night
when we weren't looking.
Above her
on stiffened arms
I held myself, did pushups. Down
to kiss her. Up
to free my erection,
so immodest.
On the corner of the blanket
a copy of *Paradise Lost*
lay spent . . .
In those days I shat poems (I still do),
but how I read them,
how *we* read them:
taking our turns on the makeshift bed,
switching the stars on
line by line.

. . . BLINKING / PUPIL-DIMMED IN A WORLD TOO BRIGHT TO BEAR.

And the rib, which the Lord God had taken from man, made he a woman, and brought her unto the man.

Under the Fifth Rib

She awoke eye-crusted and blinking
pupil-dimmed in a world too bright to bear
and thrilled to hear her own heart
thrumming birdlike and
unchained in her chest.

And it was the sun
with its long-fingered hands lifting
her leg and breast and long, golden
belly undistended
unimpregnated

unimagining the thick tangled
disgorge of humanity she would bear.

At her movement
he awakes, blue-eyed and rib-aching
to see her rise

and the hands that would carve out Abel's tomb
close in unworked,
soft-fingered fist

about her wrist.

. . . I SEE HER BODY, / BARE AND BEAUTIFUL / AND NOT ASHAMED . . .

When I Do Go on My Honeymoon

Afraid
but not afraid
to let her touch me,
we'll undress
slowly like
passing the sacrament
and when I see her body,
bare and beautiful
and not ashamed,
I'll kiss her mouth as if
she were the only woman
who ever existed.

AND THEN CAME THERE THE SNAKE / TELLING THEM TO PARTAKE . . .

We may eat of the fruit of the trees of the garden: But of the fruit of the tree which is in the midst of the garden, God hath said, Ye shall not eat of it, neither shall ye touch it, lest ye die.

Original Sin

Now, Adam and Eve
(at least, we believe)
were the first man and woman
on Earth.

They had no effects
for there yet was no sex
and with no sex there wasn't
no birth.

And then came there the snake
telling them to partake
of the fruit—which they both knew
was bad.

But they did, and that sin
allowed sex to come in;
for which thing I at least am
quite glad.

"YOU SAY SUCH VERY PLEASANT THINGS," SAID THE SNAKE.

And the serpent said unto the woman, Ye shall not surely die: For God doth know that in the day ye eat thereof, then your eyes shall be opened, and ye shall be as gods, knowing good and evil.

Blood-Red Fruit

Satan and the snake had watched each other for a long time before either spoke. It was mid-morning—it was always mid-morning—and the breeze was pleasant and warm in the thick tangles of shining dark leaves. The snake, a long purple shadow, was hanging in negligent coils from a branch of the tree hanging with blue-spotted white flowers and dark red fruit. Her large head rested on her casually muscled form and she watched Satan, who was sitting on a rock in a dusty clearing, rubbing his shoulders where his large black wings sprung, grimacing from time to time and keeping a close eye on the snake.

It was Satan who spoke first, after his grimaces and rubbing had finished. "You are very beautiful," he said.

The snake stirred, blinking. "How can you know what beauty is?" she asked. Her voice was low, and modulated. "Only the gods know that."

Satan shrugged. "I don't know how I know, snake. I only know *that* I know—and you are very beautiful."

"Are you a god, then?" Her voice was cool and musical, like a brook, and she regarded Satan with cool eyes.

He laughed, leaning back into his wings and grabbing his knees. "Do I look like a god to you?"

"You look like half a bat," said the snake as she eased down from the tree. "The other half might be monkey, might be man. You have more hair than the other two-legs in this part of the tree-place."

"Not a god though. That's a relief," said Satan. He leaned forward slightly and studied her as she moved from under the shadows of the trees. "You *are* beautiful—look at you in the sunlight. You're like a living bruise."

"What part of creation is a bruise?" asked the snake.

"A very beautiful part." Satan's mouth twitched into a smile.

"Only the gods know beauty," repeated the snake. "When this tree-place was created, the gods called it Beauty, but no creature may know what that means. Beauty is a mystery of the gods."

"It's a mystery, I will grant you that," said Satan. "To be honest, I'm trying to figure it out myself. It's one of the reasons I dropped down here—I thought it might give me some ideas."

The snake regarded Satan with deep interest. "Do you know beauty? Can you see it?"

Satan's smile was long and white. "Everywhere, no-legs. This is a beautiful garden."

"I see you are playing a game with words, then, because this tree-place *is* Beauty—and therefore beautiful." The snake twisted herself back upon her mighty loops to rise to Satan's seated height. "And I am part of Beauty, and therefore beautiful—this is what you mean?"

Satan laughed. "I did not expect you to coil me in my own words. But here, I've given you a compliment and I expect it repaid—do you think *I'm* beautiful?"

The snake shook her head. "I don't know *beauty*. It is a mystery of the gods. I do know you are made well—as the gods made you—and therefore you must be beautiful."

"A true compliment. Yet I can't imagine that anything—least of all myself could be more beautiful than you are," said Satan.

The snake blinked. "This is a new thing you have said." She thought for a moment. "How can something be *more* beautiful than something else? Both things are made by the gods."

Satan shrugged. "Personal preference, I suppose. I'm sure the gods think everything is as beautiful as everything else. I just find you more beautiful than—say, that rock over there." Satan pointed to a rock jutting from the muddy earth, crumbling and charred-looking as a burned stick. "It looks as if it tumbled from Heaven, doesn't it?"

"I don't feel more beautiful than the rock," said the snake.

"*That* is because you are a woman," said Satan, "and—innocent or not—some things breed true."

The snake blinked at him.

"Don't worry," said Satan. "It's just a joke. And not a very good one, either."

"You use words I don't know," said the snake. "What is a *joke?*"

"Just—" Satan waved his arms helplessly. "Something that doesn't mean anything."

"Why say it then?"

"Well—rather, something that means only the pleasure of saying it."

The snake thought this over for a moment, sinking back into her coils.

"Sometimes I follow a monkey, quietly, as silently as I can. I try to see how close I can come before he notices I am there. Sometimes I think of catching him in my coils. There is no reason for this that I can see, but it is pleasant to me. Is this what you mean by *joke*?"

"That seems close enough."

"So, you follow me with words, telling me things that don't matter, and *aren't* really, because it is pleasant to you?"

Satan smiled. "Hopefully, it's pleasant to you as well."

"The sun is pleasant," said the snake. "I don't know about *words*."

Satan laughed again. He had a warm voice, round and full. "Perhaps words don't know about you either."

The snake shook her head and tasted the air. "Know of me? Is this another joke?"

Satan stirred. "Beg pardon?"

"'Perhaps words don't know about me'? Can words *know*? Do words know about you?"

Satan scraped his tongue between his teeth. "No. Words do not know me. I only speak them."

The snake stuck her tongue at him, tasting the air uncertainly. "You say things I cannot understand. You say only what you are not."

"I am not more things than I am."

"That may be. I have never considered what I am not."

"Why should you? You are beautiful, and beauty—at least, for me—is its own argument."

The snake turned away at this, and for a minute there was silence. Together they watched a mouse run through the snake's coils, pick up a small seed from the ground beneath her mighty loops, and run off again.

"What *are* you then?" asked the snake. "Do you spend your days looking for beauty the way that mouse scampers about to find her food? Is beauty like food?"

"It can be." Satan sighed and gazed at her as he considered a reply. "I'm not much like a mouse, though." He rubbed a hand through the hair on his neck. "Do you know the lions with their great curved claws, their heavy coats, their sharp teeth?"

"They are creatures of the far-tree place." The snake tipped her angled head and regarded him.

"Yes. Have you seen them eat? Snapping at the straw, losing most of it because their teeth are too sharp?" He sighed. "That is what I am, I guess—a lion with teeth too sharp to be satisfied with the food I am given."

"But how could the gods make a creature that isn't built for itself?" asked the snake. "Surely that is a very large joke."

"Yes," said Satan. "Very large." He sighed again. His face distorted into a grimace and he returned to rubbing his shoulders.

"What is different?" asked the snake, confused at his expression.

"I've been flying a long way, and I'm tired and sore."

"*Tired* I know," said the snake. "One time I went from one end of the tree-place to the other, where the lions are. It was marvelously stretching." She flickered her tongue at him. "This *sore*, though—that I don't know."

"I can show you, if you like," said Satan, smiling. "But I have to warn you, you won't like it."

The snake hissed with laughter. "You're full of new words! What is *like?*"

Satan laughed along. "Let me explain, if I can. Is the far end of the tree-place much different from this end?"

The snake nodded. "Yes, far different. The flowers there are blue, and the trees have no fruit for eating, and there are more grasses. The creatures have long legs and great necks and they run in straight lines, in the way birds fly."

"So, if you were there, you might wish to be here?"

"Why, I suppose," said the snake. "But if I wished to be here, I would come here."

"And so you would," said Satan. "But say you were trapped there and couldn't come here?"

"That *would* be vexing," said the snake. "Like being caught on a rough tree branch, or in a too-small den under the earth, with all your muscles jumping to move forward?"

"Just so," said Satan. "But it would be the muscles of your inside that would be straining to move."

"You say things I've never thought of before," said the snake. She coiled at Satan's feet and rested her chin on a loop of her mighty spine, looking up at him with her black eyes. "There are muscles below muscles, and so a feeling deeper than feeling?"

"I *think* so," said Satan. "At least, it is the case with me. It's how I know I want to stop and see what is in *this* place and not in *that* place. My muscles don't know it—I know it, without my muscles. I simply *like* it."

"This is a very new thing," said the snake. "I've never heard it said before, not even among the birds, and I thought they knew everything. And so *sore* is like being trapped on the far end of the tree-place, unable to return where I *like?*"

"Perhaps," said Satan. "A bit."

"I think I should like to know what *sore* is, even though it sounds disagreeable," said the snake. "It seems that it would help me understand the far tree-place, where the creatures speak a quicker language I don't always understand."

"If you ask me, then," said Satan, and reached down and gathered the snake into his arms, the great purple coils draping his arms and shoulders. Grabbing at the snake's wide body, he gave it a vicious twist with his wrists, turning the smooth skin about on the layers of muscle. The snake snarled in a wide hiss and opened her hood at him, and Satan dropped her hastily.

"That's *sore*," said Satan, climbing back up on his rock and looking wary. "I said you wouldn't like it."

"I *don't*," said the snake, her hood still half-raised. "How unpleasant! And, quite the strangest thing, I wanted to *bite* you for showing it to me!" She nuzzled the offended section of her body. "Does sore make creatures forget what is food and what is not?"

"If you bit me, I would have been very sore indeed," said Satan. He was balanced on the triangular top of the rock, his wings outstretched for flight. "It might have been the last thing I ever felt."

"If this is how your wings feel, then I—think it should not be," said the snake, sounding confused. "Did you know your wings would feel this way if you flew here?"

"At about the seventh day, I knew," said Satan with a half-smile.

"I do not understand you," said the snake. She unfolded herself with a little shake, her hood falling loose. "Why would any creature want to feel *sore*?"

"What if you knew that feeling sore would help you understand beauty?" asked Satan.

"Oh, you make another joke." The wind swelled slightly and the glossy green leaves billowed out among their trees. "Only the gods know about beauty."

"That may be." Satan sounded tired. He eased himself back down upon the rock, sat facing the far-off sun. "But the gods made beauty to be enjoyed, surely."

The snake nodded, but her eyes were uncertain. "Only the gods know Beauty."

"Yes, but they created the world for you—and all creatures—to enjoy. And the world is beautiful."

"Yes. Beauty is its name."

"Precisely. But *sore* we do not enjoy. We enjoy beauty, but we do not enjoy sore. We do not like sore. We are not meant to like sore."

The snake tasted Satan on a passing breeze. "I think I understand."

Satan touched the snake where he had twisted her. She flinched briefly, but the sore feeling had changed. With his other hand, Satan gestured behind her. "The fruit is very red, isn't it?"

The snake turned her head to look. "That is what tree-fruit is," said the snake simply. "It is given us to eat."

"You eat the fruit?" asked Satan, looking surprised.

"Of course. I eat what all snakes

eat: fruit, berries, the seeds of the wide trees."

"How does the fruit taste?"

"Taste?"

"The feeling—in your mouth. Is it *like*? Is it *sore*?"

The snake pondered, the only sound the slight, wet flick of her tongue. "It is food—" She hesitated. What has it to do with *like*? It is not sore . . . "

"What would it take to make it *like*?"

A shadow passed over the snake and Satan turned his eyes up. As he watched, an eagle flew by again, its black eyes upon them.

"I think," said the snake. "I think I would *like* the fruit, if it were warm, like the sun, here, on my scales."

"Yes," said Satan. "I think I feel what you feel."

"And I *feel* more for you, half-bat. It is as if you are more of a snake, now that I know *sore*. Perhaps I *like* you. Is that very strange?"

Satan laughed softly. "No. It is the most natural thing in the world." He stroked the heavy rounded scales between her eyes with a long finger. "Do you understand the far tree-place better, too?"

The snake shook her head. "There are not many snakes there. The creatures have great hooves of stone and we let them roam the flatter lands alone. There is room enough in the trees and in the smaller grasses."

"Yes. The garden is large. There is a place for almost everyone." Satan's gaze lingered on the horizon. "Tell me—if you were to build your own garden, what would be there?"

"Is this a joke?" asked the snake, winding around Satan's arms so that she could rest on his shoulder and look into his eyes. "No, I see it is not a joke, though you talk about something that may be and yet isn't. My own snake garden, is that it?"

"If you like. Everything for you."

"Why would I think of another place when this place has everything there is? But I see your mind likes to see things that are beyond what is really there. Does that come from flying above the earth?"

"That might be," said Satan. "Sometimes I fly too high, or too far."

"Then you should be careful not to be too *sore*," laughed the snake. "But if I were to make a snake garden, then the snakes would also fly, so they could see the things the birds see." The snake's head slid into the hollow of Satan's throat, lay heavily near his heart.

"Do you want to fly?"

"There is another word, *want*," said the snake. "Does *want* mean a stretching of the inner muscles?"

"Yes. I think so."

"Then yes, I *want* it," said the snake, unwinding herself to loop back and around Satan's shoulders. "I would like to see the far tree-place and this tree-place all on the same day, and have the eagle's sharp eyes to see the smallest creatures under the trees. But it cannot be, since I have no wings, so it is a joke and nothing more to think of it." The snake hissed merrily. "How pleasant, to think of a snake with wings!"

Satan laughed. "It's strange that the gods did not think of it."

The snake regarded him, her black eyes sharp. "But the gods thought of everything, they say."

"And yet—" Satan said with a wink. "—they never thought of a snake with wings, for surely they would have wanted to create such a very pleasant thing."

The snake laughed. "I see now that you're trying to trap me in my own words, like clever briars. But still, the thought of a snake with wings is a more pleasant thing to me than any-thing I have ever seen in the real world." The snake sighed, and felt the edges of Satan's shoulders be-neath her belly. "Is this what is meant by beauty?"

"You would be very beautiful with wings," said Satan. "Great purple wings, dripping with warm feathers and long, strong pinions to ride the swelling winds with." His hands ran along the snake's spine as would around his torso and legs. When they passed along the spot he had made sore, she noticed that the feeling was new.

"You say such very pleasant things," said the snake. "I very much *like* lis-tening to you. I would rather be here with you than anywhere else in the tree-place."

Satan smiled. "It has been a long, long time since that was said to me." Cupping the snake's head in his hands, he said, "I think I become a little more snake, as well."

The snake tasted his nose with her tongue. It smelled of something warm and sharp.

"Your smell reminds me of *sore*, but makes me feel *like*," she said. "How is it that you make me feel things as quickly as you give me the words for them?"

Satan shrugged. "Perhaps the feel-ings were always there, and you just needed the words for them."

"And you will tell me more words?"

Satan smiled. "I'm afraid I haven't the time. I was just resting my wings." He turned his neck to rest his cheek on her scales. "I am going to build my own garden, and I wanted to see what beauty was here first."

"Your own garden? For half-bats?" asked the snake, rising to look at him, nose to nose.

Satan nodded. "For whatever ones will want to be there."

"I see now that *want* is another word for *sore*," she said. "You will not be here, and I want you to be here. That makes my inner muscles feel like *sore*." She thought for a moment, her tongue flicking in and out. "I do not like this *sore*. It makes me want to bite you in your inner muscles."

"I'm sorry you're sore," said Satan.

"What is *sorry*?" The snake untwisted herself from Satan and pooled on the rock beside him, watching him earnestly.

"Another word for *sore*, I suppose," said Satan. "My inner muscles are sore because yours are."

"So much sore! Can there be an end to it?"

"I hope not," said Satan quietly. Leaning forward, he tasted the snake's head with his tongue, and blessed her. "Little snake, I must leave you—but I do hope we'll meet again."

"What is *hope*?" asked the snake, but at that moment the wind came up and Satan spread his wings and leapt into it, laughing.

"Hope is marvelously stretching!" he called, and then with a "Goodbye, no-legs!" he sped across the sky, his great, sore wings pulling at the air.

The snake sat on the rock for a long time, watching where Satan had flapped away to his new garden.

It was not until long after that she noticed that another creature had wandered into the clearing—another two-legged one, like the half-bat, though without his great wings, and smelling of female. The snake regarded the creature evenly. The creature stood awkwardly but purposefully, her head to one side, her gaze gently scrutinizing the tree the snake had so recently hung from. With one finger, she stroked a dark red fruit and watched it swing slowly from its branch.

The snake saw something she had never seen before. "You are very beautiful," she said.

Eve turned to face the snake, startled. "How can you know what beauty is?" she said, ducking her head with a slight blush. "Only the gods know that."

. . . AND THUS ALL PEACE ON EARTH WAS ENDED.

And he said, Who told thee that thou wast naked? Hast thou eaten of the tree, whereof I commanded thee that thou shouldest not eat? And the man said, The woman whom thou gavest to be with me, she gave me of the tree, and I did eat.

Genesis

In the beginning, there was he.
He plucked his rib and gave us she.
She plucked the fruit the snake recommended;
and thus all peace on earth was ended.

Now wars and trials crimp the mirth
of all the hes and shes of earth.
Yet not one of the hes suggest
to keep his rib inside his chest.

. . . I WILL HERE RESOLVE / TO NOT BLAME YOU FOR BLASPHEMY AND BLIGHT . . .

Genesis 3:16

Unto the woman he said, I will greatly multiply thy sorrow and thy conception; in sorrow thou shalt bring forth children; and thy desire shall be to thy husband, and he shall rule over thee.

Capitulation: Forbidden Squirming

In sorrow shalt thou bring forth children. Right.
It's not your fault, and I will here resolve
to not blame you for blasphemy and blight
and mindless war and problems to be solved
by children we'll give birth to. (Ouch.) Unwise
misogynistic God did this, and sex
could have been fun without! but thirty Y's,
who never can tell what to do with X,
prefer me to unsquirming here remain,
their masculine embarrassment respect.
(I have not seen you till the earth in pain,
so why must ours be socially suspect?)
    If hearing me speak of the Feminine Mistake
    makes you uncomfortable—well. Try to ovulate.

IT HAD BEEN MUCH EASIER BEFORE THEY ATE THE FRUIT.

Therefore the Lord God sent him forth from the garden of Eden, to till the ground from whence he was taken.

How Long Till Two Times

The angel was having a hard time explaining the concept of a year to Adam & Eve. Having lived so long in a place with no time, the idea of things *changing* with the passage of *what?* What do you mean *passage?* was as foreign a concept as death or childbirth or burnt sacrifice, concepts the angel had tried to explain on earlier occasions. He sighed and looked heavenward, but he knew that they were his problem—at least for the moment.

"Okay, it's like this: right now I'm saying lalala. Now I'm not. Time has passed."

Adam & Eve looked at each other. "Uh-huh."

"Do you understand?"

"Sure . . . "

"Look, now I'm here with you. Soon I won't be."

"Soon?"

The angel sighed. It had been much easier before they ate the fruit. Back then he'd only had to check up on them, make sure they weren't choking on bark or anything. Easy. So far the only advantage to come of the fruit that he could see was that they could *finally* have a conversation without an accidental bump leading to a groping session. The modesty thing was wonderful.

"Okay," said Adam, "so when you say lalala, that's now; when you're not here that's soon. Got it. But when is a year again?"

Sort of have a conversation.

"No, no, no. 'Now' is whatever we're doing right . . . now."

"So now is just so long as you're doing something? What's when you're not doing something?"

"That's soon," Eve reminded him.

"Oh, right."

The angel uttered a brief prayer. "Look. Now is what is happening while it is happening."

"But it's always now then, because things always happen when they happen."

The angel wasn't sure whether or not this meant she understood. He decided to be optimistic. "Right. It *is* always now."

"So when you said what you said, that is now."

"That *was* now."

"But you did it when you were doing it!"

"Yes, but I'm not doing it now."

"But it *was* now."

"Right, it *was*, but it isn't anymore."

Eve looked to Adam for help, but he just shrugged.

"Let's try year again," offered the angel. "Now I'm here, later I won't be, later yet I will be again." He paused to let them consider that. "Either I'm here or I'm not. As I come and leave, time passes. After, say, a hundred times, that might be a year."

"Hundred . . ." said Adam.

"Ten tens," said Eve.

"Oh! Right!"

Hundred had been hopeless until the angel had hit on the ten tens explanation, and once that clicked they were able to grasp the idea of larger numbers with ease. The angel had, however, given up on zero.

"So," said Adam. "A year is a hundred times all together. A time is you coming and going. So, as you come and go, times pass. After a hundred, that's a year."

"And," said Eve, "when you're here is now and when you're gone is later. So each time is made up of one now and one later."

Adam & Eve looked very satisfied with themselves, and their construct *could* be useful in explaining the passage of time, and the counting of days and months and years, but it was still wrong. "Well," he said, "not exactly, but close. We'll fix it later. Now let's talk about counting time."

"Like the rocks?"

"Basically. We'll use the same numbers, but, of course, you can't see time."

"Yes you can," said Eve. "Either you're here or you're not. We can see that."

"Right. You can . . . Okay, look. Let's call now zer—one time."

"But we know it's now. You're right there."

"Just listen, all right? It's one time. Then I leave."

"Later!"

"Sure, later, whatever. Then I come back and that's two times."

Adam & Eve nodded, but the angel knew from experience that of itself, nodding meant nothing.

"So if at two times I say, 'Look, at ten times it'll stop raining for five times, so you need to gather water to drink,' what would that mean?"

Eve raised a hand. "Why would you tell us at two times? Why not at nine times?"

"That might not give you enough time—times—to get all the water."

"Well, just don't come back till we have it. You can see us."

Again, the angel wasn't sure whether to call this progress.

"See, that's the difference between me and real time. Real time goes on and on at the same speed no matter what I do or you do or anyone does."

"Except God."

"I . . . don't know."

Eve looked smug.

"Anyway, take the sun. No, the moon! That's better. You've noticed it's getting larger?"

"Yes, 'the lesser light to rule the night.'"

"Right. Well, after a while it gets smaller again. And it does that getting larger and smaller the same speed all the time. So! From the time it goes from big to small and then all the way back to big again, that's a time. Er, a month. We call that . . . that *kind* of time a month."

Eve nodded. "So when the moon's getting big, that's now, and when it's getting small, that's later?"

"Wait," said Adam, "why did you go on and on about you coming and going if you aren't time? What's it called when you come and go then?"

"Me coming and going."

"I don't get it."

"I do," said Eve, "Now and later aren't time at all, see? Now just means to be coming and later is what it is to be going."

"Ohhhhh."

The angel sighed. How could they be so clever at figuring things out so wrong? "Please pay attention. You really need to understand what a year is, because in a few *months* it's going to get cold."

"Cold?"

"Cold is . . . never mind about cold. Just know it's something bad. And *everything's* going to get it."

Adam frowned. "Get what?"

"Cold!"

"But if cold's bad," said Eve, "we just won't let it happen. God put us in charge here."

"No, no, no." The angel pushed the heels of his hands into his eyes. "Cold's not bad like sin, I just mean you won't like it. Like when you dropped that rock on your hand, Adam. The rock wasn't evil. Cold's like that—it's not evil, it just happens."

"Not if I'd known to move my hand first."

"You didn't know," consoled Eve. "But now we know about cold, so we don't have to let it fall." She turned back to the angel: "How do we keep it up?"

"Keep it up? The cold? You can't!" He pointed at the sun. "You see that? You see that sun? It's going to get farther away! You know what it's like to sit in the sun? Well, when that feeling's gone, that's—"

"Later," said Eve.

The angel nodded. "I'll be back . . . soon."

"Later," corrected Eve.

"Right. Later. I'll be back later. I just need to go . . . think for a while."

Adam & Eve watched the angel ascend, then sat down next to their altar.

And wondered how long till two times.

. . . ABEL / BROUGHT FLESH TO THE TABLE.

And Abel was a keeper of sheep, but Cain was a tiller of the ground.

Sing the song of Cain and Abel:
Cain grew grain.
While Abel
brought flesh to the table.

Their lifestyles underscore the fable:
Cain could maintain grain.
But Abel
took food unsustainable.

Then Abel, Cain murdict.
And what is the verdict—

jealousy, heroism,
or the first eco-terrorism?

AND, NO END TO HIS TROUBLES—THE BOAT NEVER SUNK!

There went in two and two unto Noah into the ark, the male and the female, as God had commanded Noah.

On the Ark

Noah had
two kangaroos
who suffered hunger
pangaroos
no matter what he
brangaroos
they didn't give a
dangaroos
till Noah wished to
hangaroos
or feed to tiger's
fangaroos
or get a gun and
bangaroos—
still,
they didn't give a
dangaroos
those pesky, picky
kangaroos.

(And, no end to his troubles—the boat never sunk!
How *is* it a wonder that Noah got drunk?)

. . . ALL WE COULD DO WAS HEAP THE BODIES TOGETHER.

And all flesh died that moved upon the earth, both of fowl, and of cattle, and of beast, and of every creeping thing that creepeth upon the earth, and every man: All in whose nostrils was the breath of life, of all that was in the dry land, died.

Along with the Rainbow

It was born when they were building it, you know. And I was just a boy—about your age, I guess—when my grandfather opened the doors and we walked back into the open air. Before he let us out, he had shooed out the hungrier, meaner ones—to clean things up, he said. I didn't understand then, but— I wish he had never said it.

Anyway we left and the air was fresh away from the animals—remarkably free of flies—at least, at first.

In some places, the sharks had done their work, but the first path I walked down with my mother—

I know why your father wishes me to tell you this, but—

It was horrible, my boy.

I was too young then to understand why the people needed to be destroyed (I may be too young still) but the lesson was clear: The Lord God is a jealous god.

There are still places—you will find them as you grow older—where all we could do was heap the bodies together. Goats and bears and aurochs, and smaller animals too, as well as the bodies of mothers, brothers, sisters—

My friend, Joey, he was my age, I saw him drowning in my dreams until I was— Heard him—

Sometimes I still—

Do you know why you're here?

Yes, yes. Of course, your father. But no, I mean— You're here because God loves you. Do you know why he loves you? Yes, well, you should tell *my* grandfather about that. Naughty boy. Heh. So like your father.

Wait, wait, wait. One more question before you go back to play. How do you know the Lord God loves you? Yes, very good. You're a smart boy. But, next time you see the rainbow, I want you to also think of the piles of bones. And the flies, and the smell—

Just—

Along with the rainbow, my boy—

Along with the rainbow, remember the bones.

"Ho, there," said the man, noticing him. "The world's gone to hell."

Up, get you out of this place; for the Lord will destroy this city.

Out of Heaven

The behemoths were screaming in panic, heaving their great shoulders at the walls of the Imperial Courtyard, their mighty necks straining at their expensive copper collars. Behind them, white birds were dashing into the blue skies in panicked bursts, alighting in trembling confusion on the ruined roofs of the aviaries. In the planters' tiers the flames burned through heavy vegetation and red terra cotta pots, billowing thick black clouds which stank and stung the eyes. Everywhere, the palace gardens were aflame, and red-tinged fire dripped from the shading-eaves and crept up the ivy-strewn walls.

"Water! Water!" The cry ran up and down the palace steps, seemed to shiver in the baked brick itself. The royal families were fleeing in a ragtag surge of emirs and secretaries, heavy purple tapestries held over their heads. The cedar door frames they passed under sagged with the weight of burning brick and fire-rotted supports; from time to time a section of the passageway collapsed in a brilliant burst of ochre flame, and an entire section of the family was silenced in a rubble-strewn roar—kings, queens, cousins, advisors, hangers-on. The porters held the long tassels of the tapestries from the flames— the slightest spark of the eerie, sticky fire and no amount of beating could put it out as it ate greedily through fabric or flesh.

The pillars of the aqueduct came down—the behemoths had found a weak spot and broken through. The brick stacks came clattering down sideways into the flame, dropping their precious water onto the flames which hissed and spat dollops of flame. One of the royal parties was dealt a glancing blow with the flame and scattered, screaming, trailing their flames like comets' tails while the now-livid tapestry suffocated the unfortunate ones caught beneath it.

Fawzi's bare feet smarted on the hot pathways of the pleasure-garden; he was tearing at the wall that separated the royal family from the common Market Courtyard beyond. The first explosion had thrown him off his feet and scattered his wares, and he had found quick refuge in one of the guard cubicles guarding the royal perimeter—the second explosion had blasted the Market Courtyard in a great foul-smelling flower of orange, and he had rolled the only way the hot winds would allow him, narrowly missing being crunched by the collapsing wall as he tumbled into the private gardens. Now, once again on his feet, he pushed at the jumbled wall, the bricks crumbling in his hands, smearing them with red dust. "Marid, Marid," he called.

There were screams from the palace behind him, screams from the ruined market on the other side of the wall. The flames were in the willow above his head, stretching out a greedy web like a fisherman's web.

Fawzi jumped up as far as he could on the uneven pavement and fallen wall. "Marid!" he screamed toward the market.

The tree came apart with huge cracking noises, and Fawzi leapt aside, weeping. The fire seized on the ground and burned on it like oil,

spreading out toward him. Stumbling backwards, he fell, cutting his heel sharply on the upturned shard of one of the garden pots.

"Save me!" Fawzi wailed, holding the bleeding wound. It was deep, and dirty. Whimpering, he added, "Where is Marid? Help me find Marid."

A horse raced by him in a sudden clatter of hooves; it leapt the wall, screaming louder than the behemoths, its mane streaming with oily flame. A figure, dark against the leaping flames, stumbled after it, cursing.

"God-sotted beast!" yelled the man after the horse. He had a handsome, hatchet-shaped face and strong white teeth, and his eyes were very fierce. "The behemoths have broken through the east wall, there's a path as wide as twenty men, and you go running into the flame." He hurled a pot after the horse, it scattered on the pavement with a dry, sharp sound.

He was dressed finely, and Fawzi struggled to his feet.

"Ho, there," said the man, noticing him. "The world's gone to hell. Someone has been very naughty indeed." He was drunk, swaying with an odd grace.

"Please sir, please," said Fawzi. "I need to get to the market."

"You're as daft as the horse," said the man, spitting into the nearest flames, which crawled and spat back at him. "There's nothing left at the market."

"Marid is there," said Fawzi. "Our stall is on the outskirts; I'm sure he's all right. But he'll be looking for me, and I need to let him know that I'm safe."

For a moment they looked at each other, the flames dull around them, the blue sky wreathed in smoke. Finally the man said, "You can't get to the market from here. You'll have to leave the city by the east wall and circle around. I can show you where the behemoths broke through, and then you can find your Marid."

Fawzi limped forward, smiling. The man, noticing his hobbling gait, looked him over and sighed.

"Broken, then? We'll never make it if your foot's like that," he said. "It's why I needed the damned horse. The pavilion's all on fire, we have to pass under it to get to the east wall. The struts are as shaky as a colt's first legs, though—we have to get through fast or not at all."

"I can run, I don't care about the pain," said Fawzi, feeling light-headed.

"You'll have to," the man gruffed. Without looking at Fawzi, the man slid his arm under Fawzi's arms across his back and held him up, pulling the weight from his wounded foot. "Quickly then," said the man, and they hobbled forward.

They walked quickly, the man pulling and Fawzi straining.

"My name's Zafar," said the man after a moment.

"I'm Fawzi."

"You're a merchant, then?"

"Yes, I—we—Marid and I—we sell lamps."

Zafar nodded.

"Are you—a prince?"

Zafar laughed, a clear ring. "No, I keep the palace guards, manage their meals and their pay. That job is a little easier now."

"What happened to them?"

Zafar sobered, biting his lip. "One of those fireballs came down on the main contingent when they were forming to defend the outer wall under the first attack. Whoever was left went to help the royal family escape, or escaped themselves."

"Why didn't you escape?"

"I was looking for someone," said Zafar, glancing at him sideways.

"Like me? And you got caught on the wrong side of the wall?"

Zafar smiled an ironic smile. "Something like that. She lives beyond the market, so I'd hoped I could get through. I couldn't even get beyond the palace walls, though, until I saw the eastern gate."

The fire suddenly blossomed a-round a squat fur-barked palm in the gardens beside them; they flinched away from it and carried on faster.

"A woman, then?" said Fawzi, hopping on his wounded feet.

Zafar's grin deepened; he dropped his head. "Yes, a woman."

"Your wife?"

"Who keeps a wife in these days?" said Zafar. "No, she was not my wife."

Fawzi smiled. "Someone else's wife, then?"

"What is it about merchants, that they always propose the most scandalous thing?" Zafar relaxed his hold around Fawzi's side, wiped his forehead. "She's the wife of an Aramaic traveler. He is very righteous—he would kill her, I think, if he knew about us."

"Every man is righteous in his own home," said Fawzi.

"Until his house burns," said Zafar. "Save your breath now, we're near the pavilion."

The palace rose up in front of them, its enormous conical structure shattered into sharp ragged spears that clawed at the sky like an eagle's inverted talons. The stink was incredible. The smoke belched up into the quiet blue of the sky.

The pavilion was of brick, a wide circle with a domed roof, the east side of the palace resting precariously on it. The heavy buttresses resting on the pavilion's supports were grinding in a fine shower of red dust, and the roof beyond had caved in, showing fiery innards. The floor of the pavilion was clear, though, and only about thirty feet across.

"We have to sprint across," said Zafar. "Can you do it?"

"Of course," said Fawzi, pale.

"You can't," said Zafar, pulling him back to look at him. "I can see it."

"I have no choice."

Zafar bit his lip, and then in one fluid moment swept Fawzi up into his arms, catching him around the knees and shoulders. Roaring, Zafar charged across the pavilion floor.

"I can run," protested Fawzi.

"Not fast enough!" panted Zafar. Running like a man in battle, he let out a thundering cry: "For Ara, wife of Lot the Aramite!"

"And for Marid, poor Marid," added Fawzi to himself, closing his eyes.

The floor shifted beneath their weight—and the balance was too great. With an enormous, dusty screech, the palace of Sodom slid forward, and covered them from the sight of the blue sky above.

ABRAHAM REMEMBERED LIFE BEFORE THIS HELL ONLY AS A DREAM.

. . . God did tempt Abraham, and said unto him . . . Take now thy son, thine only son Isaac, whom thou lovest, and get thee into the land of Moriah; and offer him there for a burnt offering upon one of the mountains which I will tell thee of.

Abraham's Purgatory

"Father," said the boy, grasping Abraham's shoulder. "Wake up. The sun has risen and I see the mountain in the distance. We're here—we're in Moriah!"

Sharp pains stabbed at Abraham's back as he sat up. He was too old for this. They had been traveling for two days and had not stopped to set up camp last night until late, too dark to see how far they'd come. He had neither the strength nor the heart to go on. The boy's enthusiasm only made it worse.

Isaac grinned. "Come, Father, it's not far. We'll get there by noon if we leave now."

The men had already prepared breakfast, but Abraham didn't eat. He feared he wouldn't manage to keep anything down. While Isaac ate, Abraham gathered wood for the burnt offering. He laid a pile of faggots atop two small logs and tied two cords around the bunch. One of the servants began to ready the donkey, but Abraham stopped him. "Abide ye here with the ass; the boy and I will go yonder and worship, and come again to you."

"Just you and—" Isaac grunted as he strained to lift the pile of wood. "—you and I?"

"No," said Abraham. "Never just you and I, Isaac. You and I and the Lord." He turned away to hide the quivering of his bottom lip. *Please, Lord*, Abraham thought as he lit a torch in the campfire, *please let it be so*. He slid the sacrificial knife under his belt and they were off, Isaac bouncing at his side despite the heavy load of wood.

"Father?" said Isaac after they had walked a ways.

"Here I am, son."

"You have the fire, and I have the wood, but where is the lamb?"

"My son," Abraham said, "God will provide the lamb."

Three hours later, Isaac lay on a slab of stone, a log along each side of his torso, as Abraham tied the boy's hands and feet down with the twine that had held the wood. The boy did not struggle; he only looked up at his father, his eyes filled with tears and questions. "Father," he said, "I don't understand. What's happening? Why are we doing this?"

Abraham did not speak, did not look at the boy. He focused only on tying the knots. *Please forgive my weakness, Lord. Forgive my fear and my doubt.*

Please, Lord.

Please give me strength.

He lay the knife against the boy's neck and cut.

When it was done, Abraham knelt before the burnt body and wept into blood-stained hands.

"Father," said the boy, grasping Abraham's shoulder, "wake up. The sun has risen and I see the mountain in the distance. We're here—we're in Moriah!"

Sharp pains stabbed at Abraham's back as he sat up. He was too—

"Isaac?" Abraham wrapped his arms around the boy and squeezed. "Isaac!"

Isaac pulled back, his cheeks flushed red. He smiled sheepishly. "Good morning, Father. I just wanted to tell you that it's not far at all. We can get there by noon if we leave now."

"Leave?" Abraham covered his mouth and turned away as he realized what morning it was, what he must do.

Again.

Three and a half hours later the boy cried as Abraham fastened twine around his wrists. *Please, Lord,* Abraham thought, *please give me strength.*

He placed the knife against his son's neck and cut.

"Father," said the boy, grasping Abraham's shoulder, "wake up. The sun has risen and I see the mountain in the distance. We're here—we're in Moriah!"

Abraham stared at the roof of the tent. *How many times will you require this of me?*

Four hours later, he placed the knife against his son's neck and cut.

"Father," Isaac said on the fifth journey to the mountain, "you have the fire, and I have the wood, but where is the lamb?"

Abraham did not answer.

"Father," Isaac said on the eighth—no, the ninth—journey to the mountain, "you have the fire, and I have the wood, but where is the lamb?"

"You, my precious son, are the purest lamb there could ever be."

Isaac did not understand what his father meant until he lay on the stone, his hands and feet strapped down.

"Father," Isaac said on the tenth—Abraham was sure it was the tenth—day, "you have the fire, and I have the wood, but where is the lamb?"

"My son, you are the lamb."

Isaac frowned. "What do you mean?"

"There is no lamb. The Lord has commanded me to sacrifice you. Do you understand?"

Isaac nodded as tears welled up in his eyes. He went willingly, but didn't stop crying until Abraham had completed the horrible task. His sobs echoed on even as his lifeless body burned, then through the long journey back to the camp and late into the night while Abraham stared with defeated eyes into the last burning embers of the campfire.

"Father," Isaac began on the eleventh day, but Abraham shushed him.

"No questions, boy."

Please, Lord, don't make me do this.

I beg of you, release me from this hell.

Please, not again.

Abraham had lost track of how many times he'd relived this day. It felt like months, perhaps a year. He was not sure which he dreaded more—waking up the next morning to kill Isaac yet again, or waking up the next morning to find his son was truly gone.

Abraham wept beside his son's burning corpse and cursed God. He knew, though, that he would continue to obey as long as it was required of him. There was no other choice.

Why do you still test me, Lord? Haven't I proven my loyalty a hundred times over?

Isaac walked beside his father, humming a tune his mother often sang.

Is this why you blessed me in my old age, only to see if I would destroy that blessing in your name?

Abraham remembered life before this hell only as a dream. He began to wonder if he had really been commanded to sacrifice his son. Had it been the Lord speaking to him, or had he imagined it?

Surely it was the Lord.

But had the Lord really meant for him to kill his son over and over like this? Perhaps God had required it of him only once, and now the abomination was on Abraham's bloody hands.

Abraham held the knife over his weeping son and begged the Lord to release him. *Please, no more. Send me a sign. An angel, a bird, anything to tell me I can stop.*

There was no sign.

Once again, Abraham lifted his knife and tried to ignore the fear in his son's eyes.

The knife trembled.

"I'm sorry, son. There is no other way. We must obey the Lord. We—we must—" *No.*

No.

I will not.

Abraham lowered the knife to his son's wrist and cut the twine. Above Isaac's grateful sobs he heard a rustling in the bush.

Three days later, Abraham arrived home with Isaac and the servants.

Sarah sat in her tent, red-eyed and

pale. She refused to look at him. "Did—did you do it? Is my son dead?"

Abraham smiled for the first time in what seemed like years. "No, my love. The Lord provided a ram, caught in a thicket by his horns, in Isaac's stead."

Outside, Isaac chatted excitedly with the servants' sons about the adventure he'd had. His laughter was justification enough.

THE GOD IS THIRSTY, AND HE WILL NOT DRINK ME.

And they came to the place which God had told him of; and Abraham built an altar there, and laid the wood in order, and bound Isaac his son, and laid him on the altar upon the wood. And Abraham stretched forth his hand, and took the knife to slay his son.

The Sacrifice of Abram

A DRAMATIC MONOLOGUE

What do we do, my love, my only? We are here.
I have made you a bed of the load of faggots
you have borne without complaint. There can be
no blame for bearing your breast against bonds,
pulling yourself up, loin-thrusting over the altar. You
seek only to break my cords, to snap twisted strings, to
bear yourself to freedom and to life. Your voice
is too young for this hurt, too fresh to frame an
Eloi, Eloi, lama sabachthani? without cracking.
Do not ask me why, my love, the vision inarguable
declared your existence a Sin. I am too old to know,
too old to bear beyond this betrayal. I am not God.
I cannot continuously slay my chosen ones
and raise up others. Perhaps He who first cut out the waiting
rib knows, knows how to gently ease this knife-point underneath
the bony birdcage of your bounding heart, perhaps He
who knows the mercy of pain, perhaps if He
should guide my hand—

He will not. I shake;
the knife-point wobbles. He never wavers, never lies
hot-eyed and feverish in a desert night, waiting for a love
which cannot return. He has no vision of bitter beds cold-sided, or
broken hearts that don't come wobbling back to Him, pleading
for redemption. So I wait, for strange-angled messengers
bidding me halt or at least the first curly-headed ram of Spring.
This deed should find its consummation, its severing at last
of the delicate ropes that bind your head and heart together.
Yet I wait, and say it is of love. Forgive me, love, my love
to you and this, my final insult: I do not stay this sharpened
Hand for you. The God is thirsty, and He will not drink me.
                    I pray for strength
to lift the silver-swift pain over my head. There
will be no startled peace for my blood-soaked soul
at your last cry, no balm to scrub away the rusted stains
or patch the open holes. Only words, words worn warm
by centuries of fathers who have lied:

God will provide.

HELL IS BUILT FOR US, OUR OWN, ALREADY . . .

And Esau said, Behold, I am at the point to die: and what profit shall this birthright do to me?

The Excommunicate

A white-shirted man rests his hands upon my back
and says, *God is not gone.* Gone! Not *gone*, no—
a plague, perhaps, swimming spiked and warm in my blood,
clotting life-giving streams, but not *gone*. God!
What can I do but nod, throat jumping?
                                        Voices form
hymns dripping with honey and milk, and yet my
mouth is dry, cotton-furry. Prayers are redundant, anyway,
appeal to Omniscience, answers before questions. Vengeful
Taskmaster, unapproachable Father, inconsistent Judge!
There are no words for Your betrayal, no way to interject
meaning into words worn dumb by pioneer polish.

It is enough, enough, and more than enough!
I rise to seek my own, my brothers—we who are
abortions of a wilderness Church; branded bastards
from the loins of an all-too-loving God. Or, worse—
the children of the red-furred Esau, once light-marked
for salvation on our foreheads. Not *our fault*, perhaps,
we have been broken by Hunger, hunger that makes us
hunt the white-reared hart and the pounding stallion's blood.
Not *our fault*, that Brothers Jacob sneer and hold warm-handed
the steaming messes of pottage. Not enough, and yet—
it is something, something to dull the axe-sharp pain. There
are some hungers which it is better to fill than to die:
what use is our birthright then?

We crack our voices
on jokes against our God: what use, what aim? He
still holds the key to the Registers. We talk of courage
and realize we are damned with *sufficient* faith, hope. We
cannot, as did Milton's fiend, build towering Heavens
out of Hell. Hell is built for us, our own, already
brimming with brimstone, the prisons of a Love which snuffs
white butterflies from darkened woods. No help
from Him who says he bore the burden of all, no hope.

Night falls without headlights, the barreling railroad of God,
crushing and grinding its *exceeding small*, forestalls words
complaint, feeling. There is no sword I can lift to shake
and challenge star-sharp skies. No hope remains save
sliced wrists, harsh medicines, or the long slow slope
built by the bored Gods. Nothing left but to rise slowly
and pay my due, a life of pain to match the debt
of an all-too-easy adoration. God does not pity me my toil
nor the pain within my side.

O, Savior, stay this night with me,
Behold, 'tis eventide.

. . . MY FATHER, / SUDDEN HIGH PRIEST, SPEAKS HIS BLESSING.

Genesis 27:26

And his father Isaac said unto him, Come near now, and kiss me, my son.

Isaac and Esau

for Dad

My father, his shoulder touching mine,
reaches into the black coiled innards of my golden, crouching car.
With darkened doctor fingers he traces
the corrugated lines of gasoline umbilicals,
the flat bright bones of car metal,
the delicate electric tendons
branching from the asthmatic engine. His voice

thrums like the aching roar above, calls out
his litany, his grimmerie, of broken valves.

Under the heavy tutelage of his godly tone, I find
my car's rancid heart, wrapped in its clots
of oilsweat and grime.

I *twist*. Oil rains down
on head and breast and loins, while my father,
sudden high priest, speaks his blessing.
"Well done."

I bite, again, my cross-scarred tongue,
and hear, heart-hear,

for once
unchilled by pain or fright
the nature of my all-too-lambent
but not too late, birthright.

I FORGAVE, BUT FORGET / HER NAME, BEAUTIFUL SISTER . . .

*And when the Lord saw that Leah was hated, he opened her womb . . . And she conceived
again . . . And she conceived again . . . And she conceived again . . .*

I counted them as they
came—sons and daughters
who didn't count.

I counted their limbs, perfect
limbs, like their father's—
nothing so imperfect.

I found him perfect, my one
week of us, my one weak
husband. I knew, walking

steps behind him, that we
were only that week, that I would
give him and forgive him

as my father gave him
to her. I forgave, but forget
her name, beautiful sister,

in the names of my children,
in the name of the Lord
who heard me.

WHEN THEY WRESTLE / ANGELS DO NOT LAUGH . . .

Deliver me, I pray thee, from the hand of my brother, from the hand of Esau . . .

Jacob, to Esau

Brother Esau, I can tell you now
    no angel has a sense of humor;
    just a light-licked sense of small
    roses unfurling from toothlike buds,
    lizards skittering clawfirst over baking stone.
        At this, he may smile, as at a toddler's stuttering words.
You will not doubt my chin curled around his holy biceps
        and felt at home, so often had it locked
        around your red and hairy muscle
        as a child, as a youth, as a frightened and furious man.
           Strength was, I always thought, your true and unpurchaseable birthright.
You would not
    I believe
        have buckled in the searing hasp
           the holocaust
           the glare with human hands
           the body and bone of light.
You would not have unraveled in the joints and limbs
        when his knowing fingers stroked your iron thigh.
    But I was ever, ever the sham of you; and my only hope a wriggling slide away.
Of me, our father might have said once *Truth leaves no handhold for conniving fingers.*
    To which I add this wisdom: *When they wrestle*
                angels do not laugh
                the frightening, familiar
                well-loved laugh of my brother Esau.

. . . WAS SOLD INTO SLAVERY BY HIS BROTHERS—TO A BUNCH OF HAIRY ISHMAELITES . . .

And when they saw him afar off, even before he came near unto them, they conspired against him to slay him. And they said one to another, Behold, this dreamer cometh.

How to Get Over It

a public service message

The Joseph Method.

Joseph, who later would use the stage name "Joseph of Egypt" (and, much, much later, "Joseph and the Amazing Technicolor Dreamcoat"), was sold into slavery by his brothers—to a bunch of hairy Ishmaelites no less. Years later, when Joseph next met his brothers, it is apparent that he had Gotten Over It. Except for the whole planting-stolen-goods-in-their-backpack thing, he was really very good to them. He gave them food and a house and collectible Pez dispensers for the kiddies. (Some translations interpret the Pez dispensers as "corn," but why would kids want corn?)

Now how, precisely, was Joseph able to Get Over It in regards to such a vile offence? Joseph explained to his brothers that, in his case, "it was not you that sent me hither [i.e., sold me into slavery and left me to suffer and sweat and rot in prison and then become second only to Pharaoh, no, that was no thanks to you], but God.

"God sent me before you to preserve you a posterity in the earth . . . "

The Joseph Method is ideal when, after some prayer and meditation, you discover that there was a great purpose in that hit and run in the Piggly Wiggly parking lot, or in your roommate's insatiable appetite for feta cheese (*your* feta cheese), but the Joseph method should only be applied, we feel, when God's hand was actually involved. We do not consider it prudent to blame all your problems on Him. That would be wrong.

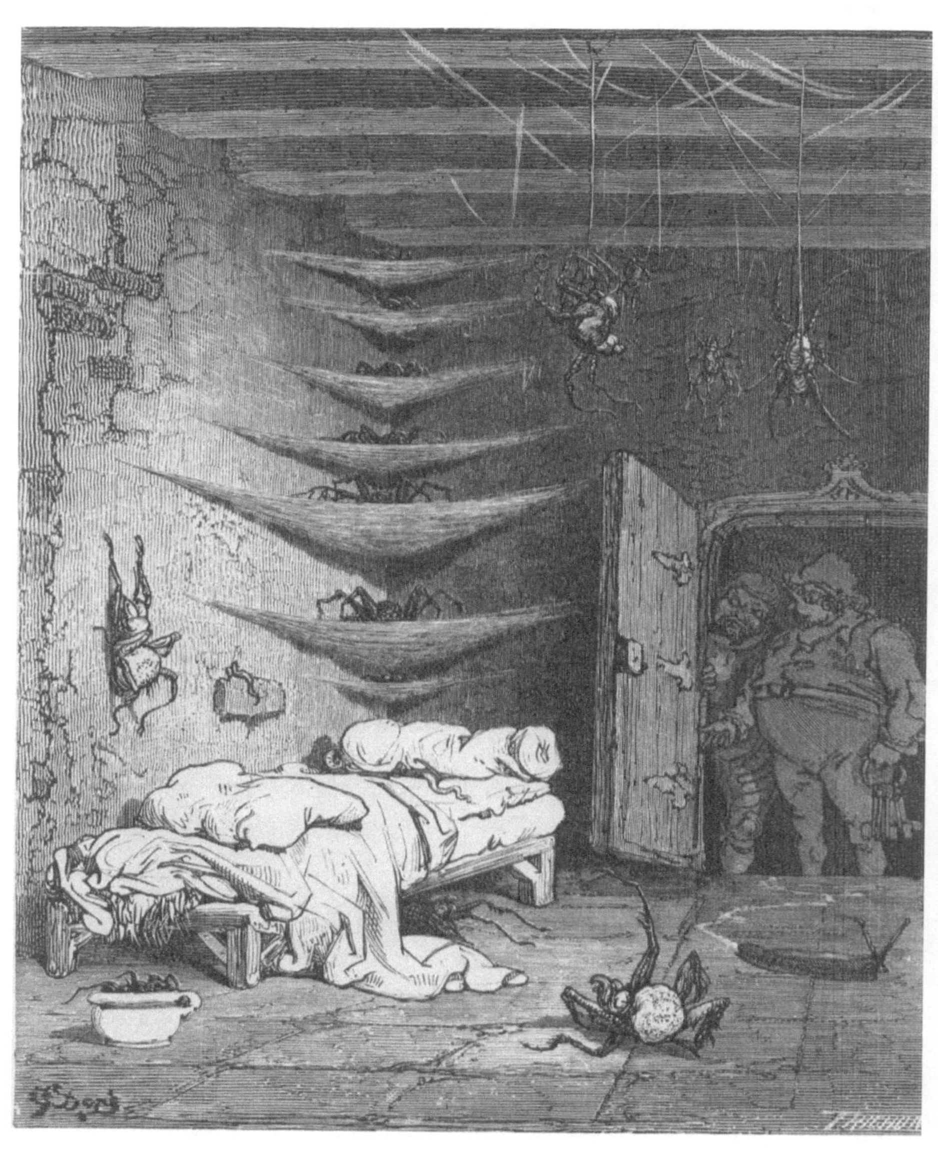

. . . THE PEOPLE HAVE FLEAS / —AND *LICE* IN THEIR HAIR . . .

And the fish that was in the river died; and the river stank, and the Egyptians could not drink of the water of the river . . .

A Travel Agent's Description of Egypt, Circa Moses

The roadways are muddy,

the water is bloody,

the landmarks half-started,

the pharaoh hard-hearted,

the cows have disease

and the people have fleas

—and *lice* in their hair—

there's frogs everywhere,

the rain is alight,

people die in the night.

So, if in your vacation,

you long for elation,

ponder awhile

before viewing the Nile.

. . . SULFURY-SMELLING AND STEAMING-MAD DOWN FROM MOUNT SINAI.

And it shall be upon Aaron's forehead, that Aaron may bear the iniquity of the holy things,
which the children of Israel shall hallow in all their holy gifts . . .

Moses und Aron

And so it was that God gave us Aaron
for Moses was slow of speech
and didn't look right in a business suit,
for we yanked on his bulrush-bred beard
and mocked him,

mocked him, the man who would that we might meet God,
lab-coated, sulfury-smelling and steaming-mad down from
Mount Sinai.
The master of the shape-shifting serpent pen—
rejected, returned the manila envelope,
advised to apply at the library.

And so it was that God gave his genius to Aaron,
the great dilutor, P.R. man of the Pentateuch,
to trim that burning bush into topiary
and punch-up the prose with a little sports metaphor,
and a little golden calf.

And so it was that we came to prefer the spokesman
while the prophet was buried in an unmarked grave
and was not permitted into our Promised Land,
where we would burn the fat of rams
and would ask God for a king.

WHEREFORE HAST THOU SMITTEN THINE ASS THESE THREE TIMES?

And God came unto Balaam at night, and said unto him . . . the word which I shall say unto thee, that shalt thou do. And Balaam rose up in the morning, and saddled his ass, and went with the princes of Moab.

Balaam's Sin

CHARACTERS

Balaam
Princes
Ass
Angel

SETTING

(Balaam is readying himself to travel. The princes of Moab, dressed fully in gray, from face to foot, stand in shadow.)

BALAAM
All right, all right. I'm coming. But keep in mind what I said: Only what my god says.

PRINCES
Only what your god says.

(An ass walks in from stage right; Balaam turns it around and mounts it, then he and the princes walk forward [toward stage right] whilst remaining in place. The scenery passes behind them, suggestions of desert hills and plains. Occasionally, in a gap, one of the princes disappears into the scenery. On they walk. Until all that are left are Balaam and his ass. Walking. Walking.)

(Balaam stops the ass and dismounts. He removes the pack and rubs down the beast. He takes food for both himself and the ass from the pack. He prepares a simple meal as the ass eats. As it cooks, he watches the ass eat. When his meal is

prepared, he sits on the ground and leans against
the ass's side. Between bites, mastication and
rumination, he speaks.)

BALAAM

It is me and you, old friend. Alone. On a mission from
man, to do the will of God.

    (beat)

God has been good to us. We have food enough to eat.

    (beat)

God has often said that those who obey his will shall
be blessed.

    (beat)

And so we have been blessed.

    (beat)

We are not hungry. Not today. Not today.

    (beat)

The Moabites are men of great wealth, you know. Great
wealth.

    (beat)

This whole land is theirs.

    (beat)

Great wealth. Almost beyond imagining.

    (He stands and cleans up.)

Excuse me, old friend. The ride has been long and I
cannot relieve myself as we walk, as you do.

    (He exits into the background. The ass settles
    into sleep. Balaam returns.)

Ah, asleep. You deserve it. It has been many a year
since we've traveled this far.

    (He pulls out blankets and leans against the ass,
    arranging the blankets around him.)

The night will be cold.

> (He settles into the ass.)

This people we are called upon to curse. They're from Egypt, you know. Now that's real wealth. Egypt! What I wouldn't do to be an Egyptian. Yet the LORD calls them a cursed people. Great be the name of the LORD. I suppose this people may be bringing the wealth of Egypt with them. That could be why they are called blessed.

> (Balaam stretches and yawns. He snuggles deeper into the ass's side.)

Perhaps, if they are instead to be cursed, the Moabites would give me of their wealth in reward.

> (He is drifting into sleep.)

. . . a blessing worthy of a prophet . . .

> (Darkness. Silence. The night passes.)

> (Morning. The background is of rockier terrain than yesterday. Balaam is awake and packing the ass. He pats it and rubs it throughout, whispering kindly. Finally he gives the pack a tug. It is secure. He stands back and examines the ass.)

Well, old friend, how do you feel? Ready to go? We head into the mountains today. You'll need the sure-footedness of an animal much younger than yourself. But never mind: the LORD is with us, as always. Great be the name of the LORD.

> (Balaam mounts the ass; he pats it gently on the neck and they are off, toward stage left, as before.)

> (The scenery is rocky. The impression is they are moving uphill.)

Rocks, rocks and more rocks. Will we ever go anywhere that is anything but rocks?

> (He urges his ass forward.)

There are lands of much greater greenness than this—there was that man last spring who spoke to us of the

land where it rains each day throughout the year. Can
you imagine the comforts enjoyed by the people of such
a land?

(Balaam looks skyward.)

Here the rain does not intend to create a wealthy
people. We are given only enough to survive. Between
us, old friend, we have spent three lifetimes tilling
the dust. And for what? Merely enough to eat.

(Scenery begins to come between Balaam and the
audience at times. He is surrounded by rocks and
crags and the occasional scrub. Everything is
dull and gray and brown and dead.)

You know what else that traveler said? He said the
LORD was unknown in those lands. He is barely known
here, I agree. Even God is restrained by the dust and
the sun! Imagine what a nation he could raise in such
a land! Why, even in Egypt there are many days when it
does not rain. I have heard they once went seventy
years without rain! But a land where it rains every
day . . . ?

(The ass comes to a halt. Balaam leans forward
and peers ahead. He strokes the ass's neck.)

This pass is no different from the last. Perhaps
narrower, but nothing you cannot manage.

(The ass does not move.)

Move, old friend. We have places to go; we are on the
LORD's errand.

(The ass begins to move but to one side. Balaam
yanks it back into a straight course.)

Don't you understand? If we do as the Moabites wish,
we can carry their wealth into a mightier nation! I
will be the LORD's prophet to the greatest nations
within his creation! A nation blessed with rains
eternal!

(The ass moves slightly to one side, then stops
again. Balaam begins to dig into it with his
heels. Hard. And again. Stabbing the beast with
his feet.)

Move! I will be great! I will carry the name of the
LORD into a new nation! A worthy nation! Not like this
forgotten land with its winds and quiet and beating
death! A land of life! Rain and wealth!

(Balaam lurches himself forward on the ass, which
staggers to one side, crushing his foot against
the upstage scenery. Balaam, enraged, lets out an
inarticulate cry, purely animal.)

(He leaps from the ass. Staggers on his injured
foot. In his anger, he breaks a dead limb from a
small dead tree. He commences to beat the ass.
One stroke. Two strokes. Three and the limb
breaks. Balaam, wild, looks about for another.)

ASS

What have I done unto thee, that thou hast smitten me
these three times?

BALAAM

What have you done? What have you done!

(He is barely coherent. His anger controls him.)

You mocked me! Me! Your oldest friend! I wish I had a
sword, you treacherous beast!

ASS

Am not I thine ass, upon which thou hast ridden since
I was thine, until this very day? And was I ever wont
to do so unto thee?

(Balaam stops. He is silent. He steps backward.)

BALAAM

No.

(A light shines from stage left, casting
everything in shades of white. Balaam falls down,
his arm before his eyes, unable to see.)

(The light gradually fades, and in its place
stands an angel glorious carrying a sword which
seems to be the source of what light remains. The
effect is of holiness. Plants and rocks obscure
the audience's view, but he does not seem to
stand upon the ground.)

ANGEL

Wherefore hast thou smitten thine ass these three times? Behold, I went out to withstand thee, because thy way is perverse before the LORD, but thine ass saw me, and turned from me, stopping before me. Unless she had so done, surely now I had slain thee, and saved her alive.

BALAAM

I have sinned. I have sinned!

(Balaam weeps.)

Forgive me, forgive me.

(He falls weeping into the dust.)

I will turn back! I will turn back!

ANGEL

Go. But the words that the LORD shall speak unto thee, that only shalt thou speak.

BALAAM

Yes, yes, yes.

(The angel rends the scenery with his sword, revealing an army beyond. Then he is gone.)

(Balaam looks up, sees the army, and stands to stare. He walks over to the ass and leans into its neck, stroking it, perhaps crying. He holds the ass's neck and it takes his weight and they stand together.)

I am sorry. I am sorry. I was blind.

(beat)

I was blind.

(He stands up and wipes his face.)

How could I have thought to curse whom the LORD had not?

(beat)

How?

(beat)

And now, now I am cursed.

(He strokes the ass's mane.)

But you . . .

(Balaam buries his head in the ass's mane as it
begins to walk forward. Balaam staggers along.
The scenery, moving also though in the opposite
direction, begins to tear. With the commencement
of the tearing, the ass's momentum becomes real,
and as the ass takes Balaam off the stage, the
tearing completes and the background of rocks and
crags collapses, revealing a mass of people on
the other side.)

An hour and a half into the jungle, the trees thinned out to reveal a lake . . .

Joshua 6:16

And it came to pass at the seventh time, when the priests blew with the trumpets, Joshua said unto the people, Shout; for the Lord hath given you the city.

The Official History

OF THE

Society for the Spiritual Attunement

OF THE

Friends of G.C. Benefield

Chapter 34

November of the fifty-seventh year pre-Cataclysm. Society Island is raised from the depths of the sea. A civilization of heathens is discovered and destroyed. A chosen nation is born.

Without a doubt, it was the most marvelous thing any of us had ever seen: Creation at work.

Our little Society, then less than three years old and hardly four dozen strong, stood gathered on the deck of the Sportsman's private yacht, the gentle waves of the Pacific Ocean lapping against the sides. It had been barely ten years since Alphaman, then a prisoner of war in Japan, had first received the revelation that would transform a brotherhood of masked crimefighters

79

into a spiritual movement destined to change our world. The Friends gathered on that yacht had experienced ups and downs together but now were at our lowest point, branded traitors, forced to renounce either our faith or our citizenship and, having made the only choice we could, left with nowhere but international waters to call our home. Adding insult to injury, we had now lost our beloved leader and would have been left to run around like the proverbial chicken with its head cut off if not for the willingness of Alphalad, a lad now in name only, to fill such large boots.

Today the young man stood before us with arms stretched wide, the golden cape of his mentor billowing in the wind behind him. "Behold!" Alphalad reached stiffly toward the heavens, the skintight white fabric of his alphasuit contrasting his slim physique with the more robust muscles of the man who had previously worn that same uniform. "Alphamen and women, f-f-friends and f-f-family." He grinned boyishly and his freckled cheeks flushed redder than his hair. He hadn't stuttered in fifteen years, not since Alphaman had found him on the streets of Cosmopolis and taken the twelve-year-old orphan under his wing. Alphalad cleared his throat, took a deep breath, and continued.

"Friends, you are about to witness the most gosh-darn amazing miracle that's been performed on this Earth in the last two millennia. Twenty-five miles behind me lies the spot where rests, on a parallel world, the headquarters of our counterparts in the League of Alphamen. Much like our Society, the League was once rejected by the nation in which it was formed. And like us, they refused to let their mission fall to the machinations of wicked men, whether those men be costumed villains like Lord Omega or villains in more clever disguises, like our friend Senator McCarthy and his House Un-American Activities Committee."

The crowd cheered a hearty "Amen" and Alphalad returned the vote of confidence with a warm smile. He didn't seem to notice—or perhaps chose not to notice—the few in back who stood silently with arms crossed, holding onto doubts in his ability to be the leader his mentor had been. The most prominent of these doubters was Sportsman, not because, as some suggested, he believed himself Alphaman's rightful heir, but because the death of his best friend still stung so strongly and it hurt him to see another wearing the white and gold. Never one to mince words, Sportsman had voiced his distrust of Alphalad's leadership ability more than once, but stayed with us, like the other doubters, because of his faith in the common goal we all shared—the greater good of all humanity.

"The League knew how to turn a curse into a blessing," Alphalad continued, "or like Alphaman used to say, lemons into lemonade. With their homes wrongfully denied them just like ours have been, they found a new home, free from the constraints of national boundaries imposed by the civilian world. From this island headquarters they fought for truth, justice, and the Alpha way until they achieved a perfect world where there was no longer civilian and alphaman, but only one people under one banner.

"So that we might bring our world in tune with theirs and bridge the gaps created by the fracturing of the universes, it is most expedient that we, too, build up a . . . uh . . . what's the word?"

Friendly laughter swept across the deck. The silent doubters in back, though, exchanged knowing glances at Alphalad's gaffe. Perhaps they had forgotten that Alphaman himself had lived and died a simple Littletown farm boy at heart, never the smooth-talking salesman the Society's detractors expected him to be. For those who accepted Alphalad as our new leader, to see him stumble now while trying to fill such large shoes was both expected and reassuring; Alphaman himself had never been particularly comfortable in his role as chosen leader of the one true faith.

"Ah, yes, an *ensign* to the nations on that very spot. But wait," he said, glancing behind himself and feigning dismay, "what's that you say? That our world is an imperfect copy of Earth Alpha, that where they have an island paradise you see before you a vast expanse of water?" He turned around now to gaze out on the ocean, his back toward us. "By golly," he said as he turned to face us again, "you're right! There's no island out there. What will we do?"

No one answered the question. Either the answer was beyond the limits of our imagination, or we feared to speak out loud what seemed no more than wispy dreams of the impossible.

"Tell me, my friends, are we helpless?"

Some muttered, not loud enough to stand out from the crowd, "No."

"Tell me, my friends, do our ancestors not tell stories of gods with great power who parted seas and raised islands up from the depths thereof?"

Some muttered a confused "Yes" while others cautiously nodded in the affirmative.

"And tell me, my friends, do men not walk among us, alphamen gifted with great Talents to rival the power of those same gods?"

The yesses rang out more strongly now. Most of us had grown numb to the miraculous nature of the powers displayed by our beloved alphamen. Sure, they could do some amazing things, but ultimately they'd been little more than glorified police officers, using Talents rather than guns to bring criminals to justice. Could they indeed be compared to the gods of myth, could they perform miracles such as those that were the stuff of legend? The very thought was awe-inspiring.

"Behold!" Alphalad raised his arms to the sky and behind us, from atop the cabin, the motor of a helicopter roared to life.

We all watched as the helicopter flew overhead, out to the sea. We strained our eyes to follow the helicopter as it grew smaller and smaller.

"Eagle Eye," Alphalad called out, "it appears that some of our friends are having difficulty seeing our fellow alphamen. How well can *you* see them?"

Eagle Eye stood tall against the rail, dressed in his buckskin leggings and purple feathered headdress, the dreamcatcher around his neck blowing in the ocean breeze. He kept his gaze fixed on the tiny chopper now several miles away. "I see our friend the Fireman has a dot of strawberry jam on his coat."

The crowd chuckled at his characteristically dry delivery.

"Dr. Twilight," Alphalad said, "do you suppose you could help our friend lend the rest of us his Enhanced Senses?"

Dr. Twilight nodded and suddenly our eyes clouded over, our view of the distant helicopter replaced with Eagle Eye's telescopic vision as Dr. Twilight telepathically broadcast his peer's perception into our minds. It was as if we were standing on the helicopter's landing gear, peering in through the windows. Aboard the copter were a pilot and four beloved founding members of the Society of Alphamen: Minuteman, the Atom Bomb, Lighthouse, and Fireman. This answered a question that had been on the minds of many, including this humble Society historian, who had noticed these four prominent Friends missing from the deck of the yacht.

Thanks to Eagle Eye's keen hearing, the voices of those aboard the helicopter were also broadcast into our minds, as if through microphones. "We're just about there," said Lighthouse to his comrades. "You ready, buddies?"

Atom Bomb shrugged his shoulders and smiled. "Sure, why not? It'll be fun."

Minuteman silently nodded while Fireman stared out the cockpit.

"All right," Lighthouse said to the pilot, "we're here. Hold us steady." He cranked open the large door on the side of the helicopter. "Friends," he yelled over the wind while gripping both Atom Bomb and Minuteman's shoulders, "it's been an honor. I'll see you back on Earth Alpha."

"No!" screamed a woman's voice from aboard the yacht, outside the focus of Eagle Eye's earshot and so barely audible to the rest of us.

Atom Bomb and Minuteman shook their companions' hands, and then Fireman gripped Minuteman in a bear hug, tears flowing down his cheeks. Their friendship had become legendary among those of us in the Society, a union stronger than blood, akin to that of David and Jonathan, Jesus and John, Alphaman and Sportsman. We could all see how difficult this temporary parting was for them both, despite their unwavering faith that they would someday be reunited as friends and brothers on Earth Alpha.

Atom Bomb dove out of the helicopter and dropped like a golden torpedo to the water far below. Immediately thereafter Lighthouse stretched out his hands and formed a dome of solid light, five miles high and ten across. The helicopter hovered over the dome, unaffected, while within the translucent dandelion yellow walls water burst up in a tremendous explosion. Fireman stood at the open door of the helicopter, tears still streaming as Minuteman stood stoically by his side. Fireman reached down and pulled the air toward him, as if tugging at an invisible rope, and in response fire and lava burst up higher out of the water, splattering against the inner surface of the dome.

"Farewell, my love," Minuteman whispered before diving off the helicopter, toward the dome. Surely it pained him to think that his longtime fiancée had chosen to deny her faith rather than leave the United States with him, but he recognized that there were greater things at stake today—greater even than love. Eagle Eye focused in on Minuteman's dive; a small hole in the dome opened to let him fall through, then closed behind him. His descent sped up as he disappeared into the flames below.

" . . . you hear me?" Alphalad's voice came into focus as Eagle Eye turned his aural attention to our leader. "Thanks, Eagle Eye. Friends, lest the importance of this moment go un-recognized, I want you to know that you've just witnessed two great—" Our young leader's voice faltered for a moment as he was no doubt over-come with emotion, but he cleared his throat and forged ahead. "You've just seen two of the greatest heroes I know sacrifice their mortal lives for our world. I'm sure this is hard for some of you to watch—as it is for me—but rest assured they've known for weeks this day was coming and they chose willingly to do this for us, for you. Also know that they are happily awaiting us on Earth Alpha and that, here on Earth Theta, Atom Bomb's wife and son will be cared for lovingly by the Society, as will Minuteman's fiancée, should she agree to join us.

"As I'm sure you've all figured out by now, our friend Atom Bomb's alphasuit protected him while he pierced the very depths of the sea, where he used his Talent to set off the largest nuclear explosion of his career. Our friend Fireman then assisted by pulling the loosened magma up to the surface, and of course our friend Lighthouse is protecting us from the force of the volcanic activity, as well as our civilian friends along the coast of South America and throughout the Pacific who would otherwise be hit by tidal waves created by the force of this explosion. All these efforts will be for naught, though, if our friend Minuteman doesn't pull off his own miracle, stretching his Talent beyond anything he's ever done before."

"You better hope he does," Sportsman muttered under his breath, though his voice was transmitted to everyone loud and clear. "If these men die for nothing . . . " He quickly faded away as Eagle Eye focused his senses elsewhere. Perhaps we were all meant to hear Sportsman's outburst, though, to remind us that feelings as innocent as concern for our fellow men, if not bridled by pure faith, can lead to doubt and dissent, even in the best of us.

The yellow dome, made opaque by the volcanic ash and soot that filled it, slowly rose out of the sea. Eagle Eye's gaze followed the gargantuan dome into the sky, a bottom forming to seal in the toxic gases as it accelerated up, up, and away. We all watched it speed toward space until it was no more than a speck against the blue sky, even to our feathered friend's Enhanced Senses. Our collective mind's eye then dropped back down to the place in the ocean the dome had covered. There was no longer lava and fire now, but a solid black mountain jutting up out of the sea. The mountain seemed to be eroding before our eyes, the crater at its peak opening toward us and widening until its lower lip dropped into the frothy depths. Clouds flickered in and out of view above the island, forming and dispersing faster than our minds could process.

"As most of you— Whoa!"

Dr. Twilight's mindlink broke as the floor beneath us jumped and everyone fell to the deck.

"We're being pulled in!" this humble historian yelled, for we seemed to be caught in some kind of whirlpool with the island at its center.

Alphalad picked himself back up. "I reckon this has something to do with the time bubble?"

"Of course," said Dr. Twilight calmly. "Water is evaporating rapidly within, so more is being pulled in to compensate. But we need to stay clear of the island—it'll be thousands of relative years still before it's livable."

The Sportsman leaped up to the bow. "Junior? You heard the man. Let's go." As usual, the crimson gladiator was more than willing to set aside philosophical disagreements when it was time to act. He jumped overboard and Junior Sportsman followed. Several of us rushed to the rail to watch as the two men—for by this time Junior, like his peer Alphalad, was clearly no longer the *boy* marvel he'd been in years past—pushed against the yacht with their mighty arms and kicked furiously to keep us in place. It was not long before Sportswoman and Sportsgirl dove in to push alongside their husbands, and then the Vermilion Streak lent a fifth pair of legs to the endeavor. It was his Enhanced-Speed kicking, raising a fifty-foot wake before us, that saved us from being sucked into Minuteman's time vortex.

Alphalad smiled. "Miracle upon miracle." He brushed wavy orange bangs off his forehead. "Now what was I saying?"

"About Minuteman," said Dr. Twilight.

"Oh, yes. As I'm sure you all know, at the beginning of his career Minuteman was able to stop the clock, as it were, for a relative minute at a time. In recent years he's honed his Talent to stretch that minute into hours or even days, and on occasion managed to turn time backwards. Usually he creates a bubble of normal-flowing time around himself or occasionally him and a few companions. What he's doing to-day—and he's been practicing for

weeks so we're fairly certain it's possible—is stretching that bubble out to the size of an island, then slowing time down outside the bubble while time passes inside normally. If all goes according to plan, a few minutes will pass out here while millions of years go by in there. And no, sadly, even with his ability to bend time our friend Minuteman will not live through those millions of years. But Dr. Twilight theorizes—and he's never been wrong before—that even after he crosses over, Minuteman's time bubble will hold for a few minutes of our time while it recedes and time inside slows to a normal pace. By then we will have—"

"Kent!" It was the same voice that had yelled before, that of the Atom Bomb's wife. She leaned against the rail, helplessly reaching for a young boy, her son, being swept away in the swift current. In a matter of seconds he was out of sight.

The crowd gasped almost in unison, then all eyes turned to Alphalad.

"Betty," our leader said as he approached her, "today your faith is truly being tested. It seems your son wanted to be with his father, and indeed he will be. Don't cry for them, but rejoice! Today father and son will embrace on Earth Alpha."

"But," she said through desperate sobs, "he didn't have a Talent. He wasn't ready. He didn't—"

Alphalad shushed her and put a gentle hand on her shoulder. "Tell me something, Betty. How old was your son?"

She wiped away tears that were immediately replaced by new ones. "Nine. He'll—he would have been ten next month."

"Well you can thank your lucky stars, then, Betty. Let me tell you something that no one here has heard before, because it's only now being revealed to me through the direct connection I have with my counterpart on Earth Alpha. When little children are born, see, there's a very thin veil separating them from Earth Alpha. That's why they're so darned smart and seem to just intuitively know these profound truths that it takes us adults years to comprehend. And that thin veil, which lasts until they're ten—remember the number ten has power, all this is interconnected in ways we don't understand—well that thin veil is like a stretched tether that, if they die before their time then SNAP! it pulls them right back to Earth Alpha. We adults have to work to attune ourselves to our Alpha counterparts, see, to develop our Talents so we can go home, but little children, they're already halfway there."

The crowd muttered in awe and gratitude. It was the connection to his own Earth Alpha counterpart that Alphalad rightfully claimed as his source of revelation, but those of us watching—even many of the doubters—saw another familiar face in our young leader's glowing countenance. Perhaps Alphaman himself, now reincorporated into *his* counterpart on Earth Alpha, was doing his part to guide his former sidekick from across the veil.

Alphalad patted Betty's back. "So dry your eyes, friend, come back here away from that rail, and don't look back. Your husband and son are gone to us, but rest assured they're in a better place. Your job now is to work toward manifesting your own Talent so you can—"

"What do you know about Talents?" Betty growled. The tears had stopped now, leaving her eyes bloodshot and fierce. "You're nothing but a charlatan in a magic costume."

Fifty faces froze in shock. Even the most doubting among us would not have so vehemently insulted our current leader or dared speak so flippantly of our first leader's legacy, the alphasuit. Differences of opinion are respected among Friends, but this was bordering on blasphemy. Even the devastation of losing her husband and son did not justify this outburst.

Eagle Eye and the Wraith moved to restrain her, but Alphalad motioned them to keep their distance. "It's okay, friends. It's nothing I haven't heard before. I admit, I'm disappointed to see such a lack of faith in you, Betty, but as with most lies, there is a grain of truth to what you say. For a long time, I *was* a charlatan in a magic costume. I was Alphalad, the luckiest boy alive, given a uniform blessed by Alphaman's Talent of the Spirit and allowed to fight by his side. With that alphasuit, just like the one I wear now, I could leap tall buildings in a single bound, stop bullets, and run faster than speeding locomotives. Like the spoiled teenager I was, I didn't understand the value of working for something because it had all been given to me, just like that.

"Even when Alphaman returned from that P.O.W. camp with his new understanding of Talents and Earth Alpha, I didn't appreciate these truths for what they were because, once again, I was riding on Alphaman's cape. I didn't have to do the work of building my own faith because I relied on his, just as I relied on his Talent. And then he died, and it was all taken away, everything he'd given me." Alphalad stepped closer to Betty so their noses were inches apart. "And you know what he told me, his final words?"

Betty stared back defiantly, refusing to move an inch. "I never should have let Flint talk me into this. You're a fraud and so was Alphaman. I don't care what he said."

We all held our breath, waiting to see how our leader would react to such blatant disrespect. He simply smiled, as a loving parent refusing to return an angry teenager's vitriol with more of the same. He placed his hand on her shoulder. "I'll tell you

anyway, Betty. 'Keep your Talent hidden,' he said. 'Keep your Talent hidden.' Can you imagine?" Alphalad stepped back and looked around at everyone, a puzzled grin on his face. "I didn't even *have* a Talent, and here Alphaman was, with his dying breath telling me to hide it. It was several months before I understood. Several months of fasting, meditation, and finally attuning myself to my Alpha counterpart and developing my own Talent. I'd long since concluded that Alphaman's dying words were a warning—that if I showed my Talent to the world they'd kill me like they did him. But that wasn't it at all. It wasn't for *my* sake I should hide my Talent, but for *theirs*, for the civilians. Alphaman had learned an important lesson about faith: it can't co-exist with knowledge. No one here has faith that this yacht can float. We're standing on it, in the middle of the ocean. We *know* it can float. Just the same, I never bothered to seek out the truth in myself and in my Earth Alpha counterpart because I had the truth standing before me in Alphaman. It was only when I had to develop my own faith that I really grew.

"Alphaman once believed that by displaying our Talents for the world to see, they would be convinced of the truth of our message and follow our example. He learned too late that casting our pearls before swine helps neither us nor the swine. We're here today building a new home away from civilization not because we've given up on the world. Rather, we come here to protect them from truths that would otherwise damn them. When the time is right, when they've forgotten the Society of Alphamen, we'll return in civilian guises and teach them the tenets of Alphamanism without revealing our Talents. Only then will they be able to learn the truth on their own, just as I did once I was forced to step out from Alphaman's shadow.

"And it's for this same reason that I haven't yet revealed my Talent. I've chosen to keep it hidden in order to give you an opportunity to exercise your faith." Alphalad gestured around him. "The fact that all these people are here today is a demonstration of that faith. I hope you can show the same faith, Betty."

Alphalad reached out to Betty but she spun away from him and leapt over the rail before anyone could stop her. The Vermilion Streak might have with his Enhanced Speed, but he was occupied alongside the Sportsfamily with keeping us all upstream. In an instant she was swept out of sight, just like her son.

Alphalad shook his head. "The tragedy here, my friends, is that now it will be another lifetime before she can hope to reunite with her husband and son. Let this be a lesson to us all that our perspective here on Earth Theta is limited, and so we must try

to see things from an Alpha perspective. Let it also be a reminder of the importance of missionary work. Who knows, maybe fifteen or twenty years from now little Christina Kane there will be teaching some young girl the truths of Alphamanism and that young girl will end up being the reincarnation of our friend Atom Bomb's poor lost wife. *Every* soul matters—even the ones you don't know, or think you don't know."

The helicopter landed back on the yacht and we all watched from a safe distance while vegetation sprung up and draped the half-crater island in green.

An hour later the yacht landed on a beach of black sand. Appropriately, Alphalad was the first to set foot on Society Island. The remaining members of the Ten followed, and then the rest of us. "On the yacht we have tents, food, and supplies to last us a couple months," Alphalad explained as he led us off the beach and into the jungle. "Once we have a feel for things, we'll head back to the mainland for more supplies so we can get started building our utopia. We'll begin with our capital city right here, and call it New Littletown."

Alphalad led a march through the strange vegetation, toward the center of the island. Lighthouse marched alongside him, clearing a path with a giant machete of solid dandelion light. Dr. Twilight hypothesized about the evolutionary patterns that had led to the unique species of flora and fauna we came across. The Streak zoomed about, placing markers where Alphalad named future sites of construction. "Over there, the library, and here, the hospital. A grocery store in that clearing, and perhaps along the stream a residential zone. How would you like to build your house right there, Sportsman?"

An hour and a half into the jungle, the trees thinned out to reveal a lake, and at the center of the lake a little green island. And on the island a great stone tower, reaching up to the clouds.

"Curious," said Alphalad, scratching his chin. "I wonder who built that? This must be the center of the island. It's right where our temple should be."

"Cover!" Eagle Eye shouted while throwing his own body over Alphalad's just in time to catch an arrow in the shoulder. Lighthouse quickly conjured up a giant shield to deflect a barrage of wooden arrows coming across the lake from the tower. Eagle Eye reached around his neck and ripped the arrow out while grunting through clenched teeth.

"Thank you, friend," Alphalad said while standing up. Arrows continued to thump against the translucent shield over us. "You know my alpha-suit would have protected me, don't you? As would yours," he said, grinning, "if you weren't so insistent on running around bare-chested."

Eagle Eye nodded. "I hear them inside the tower. It sounds like there are hundreds inside. They were expecting us—something about ancient prophecies, as far as I can tell. I'm certain it's English they're speaking, but it's no dialect I've ever heard."

The Vermilion Streak gazed up through Lighthouse's translucent shield at a window in the tower. "Are my eyes tricking me, or are there giants up there?"

"It's no trick," said Eagle Eye, following the Streak's gaze. "Those archers are each a good eight or nine feet tall."

"They're terrified of us," Dr. Twilight said, touching his forehead with two fingers. "They've never seen people from the outside world. They built this tower to protect them from the . . . the Great Statue Maker? Of course. The receding time bubble. If they saw their friends pass over to the other side, it would seem that they were frozen in time. And the bubble just kept getting smaller and smaller until they were all gathered here in this tower . . . That *is* the center of the island. Minuteman must be buried somewhere in the lava rock below the tower, at the center of the time bubble."

"Bernie's down there?" Fireman said as tangerine-colored flames gathered around his fists.

"His body, Howard," Alphalad said. "There's no way he's still alive. Remember, it's only been a couple hours for us but here on the island it's been millions of years. And Atom Bomb was at the center of a nuclear explosion and then an undersea volcanic eruption, so he can't have survived, which begs the question . . . "

"Where'd the natives come from?" Streak was zooming through the crowd of Friends gathered on our side of the lake, popping in on several conversations.

"My God," said Dr. Twilight. "That would explain their size. Between the effects Atom Bomb's nuclear Talent must have had on little Kent's genetic makeup and a millennium or so of evolution . . . They must be descended from Betty and—"

"Her son?" Streak spread the word around, then popped back in to add an "Eww."

"Who can blame them?" said Lighthouse, while keeping an eye on his shield. "From their perspective, they might as well have been the last two people on Earth. They did what they had to in order to preserve the species."

Sportsman stood with his arms folded. "Can we stop discussing the ethics of incest and do something about the people with arrows who are trying to kill us?"

"Give me a chance to communicate with them," said Dr. Twilight. He closed his eyes and concentrated while the rest of us watched. Suddenly he hunched over in pain and his eyes

popped back open, white and pupilless. "Murdrers! Die! Punsh punsh punsh must. Die die die hit ard stron craskulls feebains hu-hu-hunh—" The doctor stood upright and gasped for breath. "Ti yortsed yeht erofeb snehtaeh eseht morf dnim ruoy esaeler. Flesruoy mlac, dneirf dlo ym nats." He shook his head and blinked until his pupils returned. "They're so . . . so primitive, so full of rage. Their minds are cloudy, disorienting."

"Heh," said the Streak. "Generations of inbreeding'll do that to ya."

"I tried to reason with them," said Dr. Twilight, "but it was impossible. I wasn't prepared for such mass insanity—if not for one sane mind among them that I was able to latch onto, I might have been lost."

"One sane mind?" asked Alphalad.

"Yes, he's in there with them but he's not like them. His thoughts are entirely rational, albeit . . . backward. And he—knew me?"

"We'll have to thank him for saving you," said Alphalad. "And the others in there?"

"All they understand is that we are the prophesied Bringers of Death who would follow the Great Statue Maker. They . . . " Dr. Twilight frowned and looked at his boots. "According to their traditions, we are the evil gods who murdered their First Father."

Alphalad shook his head. "Then we've already lost them. See how lies can corrupt an entire civilization? I'm afraid their only hope now is that in their next lives they'll be willing to hear the truth and that our missionaries will find them, wherever they're reborn."

"Reborn?" Eagle Eye shook his head. "No, what you're suggesting is unacceptable. We don't kill."

"We have before," said Fireman somberly.

"That was different. He was a villain who had killed countless times and he was going to kill you."

"He did kill me," Fireman corrected. "I would still be dead if Minuteman hadn't shunted him back in time and tricked him into killing his future self in my place."

"And Alphaman approved that decision," said Alphalad, "because it was for the greater good. As it is today."

"Don't be ridiculous!" said Sportsman. "Nobody has to die today. We've got a few hundred primitives with bows and arrows. Send Streak in there and he'll have them all disarmed in two minutes."

"Hey," said Fireman, stepping in front of Sportsman, "watch who you're calling ridiculous. Alphalad is our leader. Treat him with the respect he deserves."

"Are you going to make me, you flaming—"

"Please, everyone," said Dr. Twilight, "let's all calm down and discuss this rationally. Conflict among us only takes us farther from Earth Alpha and

closer to Lord Omega's influence."

"That's right," said Alphalad. "Do I need to remind you of the lesson poor Betty O'Conner failed to learn, which is why we're in this situation in the first place?" The young man took Sportsman's arm in a loving grip. Just as on the yacht, those of us watching caught a glimpse of Alphaman in his former sidekick's countenance. It seemed Sportsman saw it too, but he turned away, as if refusing to acknowledge the boy had become a man.

Alphalad smiled calmly and confidently. "You're still looking at things with your Earth Theta eyes, Bill. Step back and look at this from an Alpha perspective. Yes, we could disarm those poor savages and send them on their way, but then what? You heard Dr. Twilight—they've had nothing but fear and hatred bred into them for generations. We can take away their weapons, but we can't take away their hate. And what about the generations to come? How many more souls will be lost because we're too shortsighted to see that these heathens must be reborn for their own good?"

Sportsman clenched his fists tighter but didn't say anything.

"Are you sure about this?" said Lighthouse. "It seems kind of drastic."

Alphalad stood tall and puffed out his chest, reminding us all of the principles embodied in the gold triangle emblazoned thereon. "The time has come, friends, for us to step up and make a real difference for this world. This tribe of warmongers that should never have existed in the first place would kill us, would stifle the all-important message we have yet to deliver to so many of our friends-to-be throughout the world. In the spot where our forebears on Earth Alpha erected the headquarters from which they led their world to peace, over the graves of our fallen friends, these abominations have raised up a mockery to everything those valiant heroes died for. We cannot let this be."

Eagle Eye nodded. "You've convinced me. This is the right thing to do, for the greater good."

"It's for their own good," said Lighthouse. "We do this out of love, even for these friends we've never met."

"Fine," said Sportsman. "Let's do it."

"For truth, then," said Dr. Twilight.

Fireman raised his flaming fist high in the air. "For justice."

And then we witnessed yet another miracle. Alphalad stepped toward the edge of the lake that surrounded the tower and crouched down. He closed his eyes and pressed his palm into the mud, just as Alphaman had done so many times before when exercising his Talent of the Spirit to commune with inanimate objects. Then, before our eyes, the water receded away from Alphalad's hand, heeding his command. The water continued to recede to the left and to the right until there was a path of dry ground leading across the lake to the tower.

Sportsman affectionately punched Alphalad in the shoulder. "Well done, Alphaman."

After rushing across the dry pathway and into the tower, guided by Dr. Twilight to rescue our new friend Backwards Man—whose story shall be told in other chapters of this history—the Vermilion Streak ran around the tower ten times at superspeed, weakening the foundations with the vibrations of his feet. The four members of the Sportsfamily then placed themselves around the tower and blew their ultra high-frequency sportswhistles, which can only be blown by the powerful lungs of an alphaman with Enhanced Strength. The resultant sonic attack from four sides at once caused the walls of the tower to crumble, burying all within. Finally, Fireman lit the rubble in a great funeral pyre that reached up to the clouds above. Like Sodom and Gomorrah and the people of Noah's time, these sons and daughters of incest and lies were wiped from the face of the Earth, that they might be reincarnated and have a better chance at salvation.

Later that night, as we set up camp on the south bank of Lake Minuteman, Fireman watched the dancing orange flames leap up to heaven. "Farewell," he said to the tower of flames. The tears that glistened on his cheeks were tears of sadness for his lost friend, tears of joy at the know-ledge his friend lived on, and tears of pride in the historic events he'd been part of. This day a great nation had been born, one that was destined to lead the world to a better place.

Some among us who were there that first night on Society Island swear they saw, in the heart of the majestic bonfire where our temple would soon be constructed, the hooded figure of Minuteman.

Some say he was waving goodbye.

Others, that he was beckoning for us to follow him to paradise.

TRUST, TRUST IN THE LORD, DEBORAH PROCLAIMS.

And Deborah, a prophetess, the wife of Lapidoth, she judged Israel at that time. And she dwelt under the palm tree of Deborah between Ramah and Beth-el in mount Ephraim: and the children of Israel came up to her for judgment.

Song of Deborah

Awake, awake Deborah. Awake, awake utter a song.
Israel's been in captive captivity twenty years long.
Arise, arise Deborah. Arise, arise mother of Israel.
Deliver them from the king of Canaan in the days of Jael.

Prophet, prophetess Deborah. Prophesies and lauds
For the children of Israel, who have chosen new gods.
War, war is in the gates. But there's no spear
Or shields to protect the inhabitants from fear.

Hear, hear oh ye kings; give ear princes this day.
Listen unoccupied highways and traveler byways.
Drop, drop heavens. Drop clouds of water and word.
Melt, melt mountains. Slide Sinai before the Lord.

Awake, awake Barak. Awake, awake this people to lead
The armies of Israel 'gainst Yavin in their direst need.
No, no, said Barak. I will not go, unless Deborah go.
Go with me and my ten thousand soldiers into the fro.

Trust, trust in the Lord, Deborah proclaims. He will lure,
The commander of Canaan, Sisera, on the way to Tabor
And give him, his troops, and chariots into your hands
And the victory will not be Barak's, but a woman's.

Blessed, blessed be the Lord. For Israel's delivering
From the noise of archers in the places of water-drawing.
Rehearse, rehearse the righteous acts of the Lord who waits
To lead the children of Israel down, down to the gates.

. . . FORGETTING ALL ABOUT Heber's wife . . .

Then Jael Heber's wife took a nail of the tent, and took an hammer in her hand, and went softly unto him, and smote the nail into his temples, and fastened it into the ground . . .

Nailed

Oh, women cannot handle tools,
says chauvinistic grammar
forgetting all about Heber's wife
and how she used a hammer.

I'M GOING TO BE A GREAT MAN AND WIN BATTLES SINGLE-HANDEDLY—
EVERYONE SAYS SO . . .

And the woman bare a son, and called his name Samson: and the child grew, and the Lord blessed him. And the Spirit of the Lord began to move him at times in the camp of Dan between Zorah and Eshtaol.

Swinging

amson is fond of fun; he's got a deer rigged up by its hind legs and he's letting it idly spin, its slender head going frantically up and down like the wheel-and-string toys my grandmam used to make for us. We're all laughing at Samson pretending to box the deer, he keeps missing and his glancing blows send it wheeling erratically, sometimes knocking it against the trunk of the tree from which it's hanging, sometimes spinning tightly back toward Samson, who grapples it awkwardly in an upside-down embrace.

"Another conquest for Samson," laughs Hod. It's his idea of a joke; he also, in a strange way, means it. He's sitting in my lap, his heavy curled-hair head resting in the crease where my arm joints into my torso. This is another idea of his that is a joke, another thing he strangely means—he will flirt with the wives passing on the dusty way to the wells only if he is in the attitude of a wife himself. I roll him off from time to time, to spar with Lior as the occasion presents itself, or to make myself more presentable for the circumspect daughters of the priest, but somewhere along the way Hod and I grew into each other, head to shoulder. He is my right arm.

Samson grins at Hod's comment, mimics sex at the deer, which embarrasses Hod and makes Lior and me laugh. Samson is slow in everything but wrestling and insinuations, and his mimicry shows practice and skill.

"Beware, Samson," says Lior on top of his laughter, "that beast is no daughter of Israel. You wouldn't want to sire bastards."

"It's the daughters of Israel that are the bastards," Samson says, flushing. "This deer has more life in it than all of them, combined."

We laugh, but less than before. Samson can woo Philistine girls and Caananite girls and no one but the very old will tell him differently, but Samson is built like a young ox, muscle on muscle. We are leaner and less famous, so we cling to our nation.

"Cut it down," says Hod, affecting a yawn. The deer is sweating, and it makes him nervous to see things suffer. "We have enough meat."

Samson shrugs, pulls out his knife and saws the beast down. The doe scrambles to her feet, weaving drunkenly. We laugh at her skittering, swaying departure, chasing her out into the desert with our voices.

Samson sits down with us in the shade of the tree, leans back into the hard, baked earth. "The women should be here, soon, for the midday wells." It's the reason why we are here and not toiling in the fields or loitering in the market. Samson pulls his heavy hair away from his neck, drapes it over his shoulder. "Baal, it's hot."

We all bite our lips, smiling lopsided smiles at this blasphemy. Samson is famous because he dares things without thinking—we cannot help but think before the jump, and that hesitation makes us small. Of the three of us, Lior is the closest to Samson, but because of this he is the most uncertain, and so when the

first of the black-hooded women step over the rise, Lior is the first to call out, "Here they come."

The women wander together in odd, clotted clumps, they are smiling and laughing; they grow somber and stiff as they pass us lazing in the dust. There is Idit, the priest's eldest daughter, severe and blushing both among a knot of her sisters, and Hod gets too hot. I push him off; he slides easily away to sit on his own.

"How goes the well-women?" shouts Samson, bellowing.

"Well enough," says Idit, barely looking at him.

"Hot today."

"Not for those who can afford to sit in the shade," Idit says calmly. Her sisters burst into suffocated giggles.

Samson puts out his teeth; it's frightening inside his weighty black beard. "Come sit with us, then."

Idit shakes her head, trying not to smile. "Who would gather the water, then?"

"Let the camels gather their own water," tries Lior, and Samson grins at him. A success.

"A camel is too stupid to do much but sit in the shade," says Idit. "And yet still they are valuable to your father, Lior Bar-Gidon. We daughters must work harder and be wiser."

We're losing them, already they're wandering, giggling and glancing, beyond the point of repartee. Samson says, easily and deeply, "If Lior and Hod help carry, there is time enough to spend resting in the shade."

This is confusing; Hod and Idit both look at me, sudden and sharp, and the rest look at Samson. I can feel heat creeping up over my scalp, but whether it's from being singled out by Samson, being caught between Idit and Hod's question-mark brows, or from my own uncertainty I can't tell. Lior clears his throat, the girls shuffle nervously. In the end, Idit saves us all; with a curt nod at Samson she says, "That would be a blessing, Samson Bar-Manoah. But water first, then rest." She does not smile, but she glances my way.

Hod and Lior leap up as if catapulted, the girls giggle again in tiny implosions. My two friends join the group, taking the girls' water-pots—they are awkward with them, Hod especially. The cluster of girls consumes them, and they proceed together, out of sight into the dust of the road to the wells.

It is very quiet between Samson and I, and the birds become loud. I am just about to say something when Samson grunts and says, "Would Idit sleep with you, if you were to ask her?"

I shrug. "I don't know. She's the priest's daughter."

Samson spits into the dirt. "That means nothing."

I can't explain that Idit terrifies me, so I shrug again, saying, "I guess she would, then."

Samson laughs at that, his teeth out. "Beware, Amnon. Women can string you up and knock you about, just like that deer. Idit would crack you against the tree trunk till your brains were broken. Women are like that."

"Doesn't seem to stop you," I say with a grin.

"Nothing stops me." He stands, stretching. He points at the dust of the well party retreating over the further hills with his chin. "Hod, you and he—?" There's a question at the end of his words.

"What about him?"

He shakes his hairy head. "Nothing." Scratching his belly, he tries again. "You're like brothers. I don't have any brothers."

"Yeah, Hod and I are brothers." We're more though; I realize it. I would weep if Hod were to leave me—loudly if he died, softly if he were to marry, the way a father might for his son.

"He trusts you." Samson's eyes are still far away. "You trust him?"

Hod is my right arm. He would carry my shield in battle, and I would carry his. "Yeah, I guess."

This gets a glance from Samson, his eyes are unaccountably fierce. "You guess too much."

I laugh; it's sour. "Why are you all upset about Hod?"

"Just—" Samson waves his meaty

hands to the sky, grasping at words. "Why Hod? Why not Lior?"

"Lior can't think of anything but girls."

Samson laughed, his fierceness dissipated. "*That's* God's truth." He sat next to me, his thick arm resting near mine, almost touching. After a moment he says, "Could we be brothers, too?"

I feel the heat all over, then—face and hands and feet even. "Um—sure, Samson. Of course." I squirm in the dust, my hands unsteady supports.

He looks at me, swift and cutting, his stupid eyes suddenly cunning and birdlike. "Don't play with me."

"I'm not," I say, my stomach crawling.

"Fine, then," he says, looking away.

"Fine." We are now both staring ahead, not daring to glance at each other.

At last Samson stirs; I pray it is to get up to meet the girls and Hod and Lior—maybe a race. But he is not rising, he's sidling over to me to rest his dark head on my shoulder, to lean against me as if he were Hod.

"Well, then, brother," he says softly, closing his eyes.

I am suddenly itchy everywhere, and my arm goes dead instantly under his weight, crawling with ghost prickles. "Look, Samson," I say, feeling strangled.

His eyes open, brown and wary,

looking up into mine, and it's too much. I pull away from him, rubbing my shoulder. "This is really weird, Samson."

"It's just what you do with Hod," he says, flushing.

"That's—that's different," I say. "That's Hod. This is—"

"What?" he says heavy and ferocious, his teeth dangerous.

"Look, never mind. I'm just saying—"

"No, you tell me what 'this' is, since you know so much." The finger he points at me seems suddenly enormous, impossibly muscular.

"It's just strange, Samson!" I say. My voice has a cringing whine.

His answer is an incredible sock with the back of his hand to my cheekbone that picks me up and sends me tumbling end over end on the hard ground. I can feel the bones in my face realign in the shock and then settle back, can feel the lines of his fingerprints pounding in flame on my face. I land in a sprawl, but before I can straighten myself he is on me, his hand gathered in the hair at the nape of my neck, his lips against my ear.

"I am *not* strange," he says in a horrible hiss. "You—*bastard*—you don't know anything. I don't care about your stupid laws or stupid women or stupid God. I'm going to be a great man and win battles single-handedly—everyone says so—

and I'm going to make love to a hundred women a day, which is more you could ever even *dream* about. And no one's going to tie me up and let me swing, no one. I'll marry a Philistine princess, I don't care—I don't care about *you*—" and he spits on my face, and knocks me against the ground for good measure. My nose spouts blood, red and tasting like iron.

He kicks at me, misses in a howling half-fall, and then is gone, pounding away across the thirsty, cracked earth.

After a moment, I pull myself off the ground, coughing. For a time I try to stanch the flow from my nose, and then there is the noise of the returning party, and Lior's laughing face falling into a confused frown, and Hod's familiar weight at my side, and above all the kind eyes and soft hands of Idit, holding me up and proffering me a sweet, cool drink of water.

. . . HE TOLD HIS SECRET TO A LASS . . .

And it came to pass afterward, that he loved a woman in the valley of Sorek, whose name was Delilah.

Delilah

Tho' Samson was a Nazarite,
he kept the ladies up at night,
showing over (and again)

the stamina of thirty men—

Still God his muscled promise kept!
And yet, one night, as Samson slept,
he told his secret to a lass
(once more, the jawbone of an ass!).

But, consider, Samson—with this I'll ply ya—
I'm going bald—*without* Delilah!

SO SAMSON ASKED GOD FOR ONE MORE MOMENT OF STRENGTH . . .

And Samson took hold of the two middle pillars upon which the house stood, and on which it was borne up, of the one with his right hand, and of the other with his left. And Samson said, Let me die with the Philistines.

How to Get Over It

a public service message

The Samson Method.

Boy, you think Joseph had it bad. At least he didn't have his locks ravaged by a bunch of Philistines like Samson. So Samson asked God for one more moment of strength and brought down the building, killing everybody.

The Samson Method is just that: kill everybody. Its drawbacks are numerous.

SHE WORRIED HE WAS HUNGRY . . .

And there went out a champion out of the camp of the Philistines, named Goliath, of Gath, whose height was six cubits and a span.

Philistina

Goliath's mother loved him.
Goliath's mother cared.
When Goliath went to Israel,
she wondered how he fared.

She worried he was hungry,
or getting bitter-browed.
She wished he were not far away.
He really made her proud.

So, when you talk of David's faith,
how he was always true—
remember, please, Goliath's mom,
and that she loved him too.

. . . AFTER THE DREAMS / AND THE PROPHETS . . .

Of the Blessed Dead

He comes doubting

> *after the dreams*
> *and the prophets,*
> *after the silence.*

He comes doubting

> *will you fail me?*

He comes doubting

> *will you wake me?*

He comes doubting

> *gods ascending*
> *out of the earth.*

He comes.

. . . IN EACH AND EVERY DAY /
ONE THOUSAND, FOUR HUNDRED FORTY LITTLE MINUTES PASS AWAY.

But king Solomon loved many strange women, together with the daughter of Pharaoh, women of the Moabites, Ammonites, Edomites, Zidonians, and Hittites . . .

Solomon's Lament

Astronomy reminds us how in each and every day
One thousand, four hundred forty little minutes pass away.
And yet, I have o'er fifteen hundred wives under the sun—
that leaves me only seconds to see each and every one!
All day they walk before me in a strict and single file.
They say "Hello" and then "Goodbye" while smiling all the while.
They all are sweet and beautiful, exotic, warm, and fun—
but *oh*, I wish I had more time to spend with only one!

HE HAD TO HAVE HER, THAT MUCH WAS SIMPLE.

Of the nations concerning which the Lord said unto the children of Israel, Ye shall not go in to them, neither shall they come in unto you: for surely they will turn away your heart after their gods: Solomon clave unto these in love.

Solomon's Reprise

Solomon stood atop his palace in his famous gardens smelling jasmine from Aramaea, saffron from Thrace, and the blossoming ume tree from Zhou. In the middle of his garden, in an elaborate pot of gold and jewels and lupis images of a sheban goddess, was his most famous flower of all. A blood-red jule rose—the sole honest one among the thousand fakes delivered him by the Queen of Sheba. As he watched it, a bee crawled from the topmost bloom. The best of omens—no matter how much that old fuddy-duddy Ahimaaz groused about omen-finding being pagan. It was like Solomon told him: God didn't come to *your* bedroom and make *you* the wisest man in the world so shut up. It was appalling how those priesthood types thought they knew more than him. No one knew more than him! He was Solomon!

Just try and find a *priest* God-chosen to build temples. No such thing. God requires a king for that. A righteous king.

But one thing was bothering Solomon. And if Hadadezer heard that Solomon hadn't managed to arrange one of his famous strategic marriages in nearly a month, well, Solomon would never hear the end of it. Damascan kings were all the same. But no matter. Even that problem should be solved before the sun dipped below the horizon. Probably before it even reached its zenith.

The small band of Oscans who had recently moved into Jerusalem had been making it hand over fist lately; the wealthy of the city were snapping up their cloth like they had never seen cloth before. And no doubt, their work was terrific. Solomon had had them redo the Holy of Holies. Of course, Ahimaaz had taken umbrage over that as well—unbeliever this, uncircumcised that. Twenty years ago Solomon might have felt the same, but these days, well, he was Solomon. And the Lord deserved what Solomon deemed the best, nothing less.

The Oscans' chief was a short and unpleasant man who, for all his brilliance, was ill-disposed to hide his filthiness. His daughter was the same, so Solomon had ordered her bathed before she arrived.

With the chief's daughter, Solomon figured he could get a pretty hefty discount when it came time to replace the harem draperies. That was going to be a massively expensive project anyway—it was totally a win-win situation.

A throat-clearing interrupted Solomon's reverie and he turned to face the young woman behind him. He had never seen her standing up before; why, she was nearly a head taller than himself! "Hello," he said, startled. She merely bowed slightly in reply. Cocky pagans. But the bow did provide a striking view of her newly clean hair. What a color! Never had he seen such a sunset! It was certainly more striking than the similarly tinted dancing whores the Illyrian ambassadors had once brought him.

At his gesture, the girl turned slowly around, the morning sun passing through the tunic the bathers had put on her and letting him examine her silhouette. Her breasts were those delightful roe-like little mini-mounds he had so loved as a young man, and from her delightfully pale skin (another pleasant surprise) he bet her nipples would be just like Anah's at this age. He doubted the little Oscan girl was fifteen yet, based on her buttocks and pelvis, but that was fine. He would have her tonight after the wedding of course, but in a couple years she would be his favorite age. He would have to tell Birsha to put her on the regular rotation come, mmm, eighteen months probably. Excellent.

That was about the time he would be looking to replace that Urartu girl. He nodded as she looked up at him. Her eyes dropped immediately. This would be a marriage made in heaven.

He felt his loins stir. Another good omen.

"Girl! You're lovely! What's your name?"

"Caíla." She bowed her head and the morning sun fell atop it like a brushfire.

"I must say, with your hair combed out— I hadn't expected— You are rather tall, aren't you?

At this she looked up at him from under her eyebrows.

Solomon giggled a little at her look—it was almost creepy how she had to look down in order to look up. He rubbed his hands together, cleared his throat. "I have compared thee, O my love, to a company of horses! Pharaoh's horses! Thy cheeks are comely with rows of jewels, thy neck with chains of gold!"

Caíla reached up and touched her naked neck.

"Behold! Thou art fair, my love—thou hast doves' eyes!"

Her head was no longer bowed, only inclined downward in order to stare at the king.

Solomon looked at her, his arms akimbo, watching her. He nodded. She frowned. He widened his eyes expectantly.

"Oh! I, uh, I am the rose of Sharon and the lily of the valleys? Stay me with flagons for I am sick of love?"

"Oh, excellent. Well spoken. Such a pretty voice. Like a bird, really. Do you sing?"

"Sing?"

"Say, 'selah.'"

"'Selah'?"

"Wonderful! I have this thing I like to do with the harem girls where we take my daddy's hym— But we'll talk about that later. In about eighteen months, I imagine." He chuckled. "Now. Where was I? Ah yes.

"Thou hast doves' eyes within thy locks; thy hair, goats; thy teeth are a flock of sheep even shorn—love

that—; thy lips are like a thread of scarlet. Thy speech is comely! Thy temples are like a piece of pomegranate—love pomegranates, ever had one? No? We got a tree up here somewhere . . . Never mind. I'll have Meshulle get you one—thy neck is like an armory of strong men. Thy two breasts are two young roes, twins, feeding among lilies—that one's so true of you, Caíla; I'd have you take that thing off right now except Daddy told me a naked woman on the roof's bad luck—; thy love is better than wine. Wine! The smell of thine ointments—get it? ointments?—is better than spices; thy lips drop as the honeycomb, honey and milk under thy tongue—"

He went on and on. Caíla watched him, her jaw dropping slowly, until the honey-and-milk line—she was no dummy; she knew this was poetry— but she didn't want him to take her open mouth as an invitation to dip into its honey. All she was supposed to do was drop off some swatches. Kings were so weird.

Besides, he might be king, but he still wasn't as cute as her cousin Leikit. That's who she was supposed to be with right now. They were going to see the baal show in Bethlehem—a troupe of Edomite actors had been there all week and everyone was talking about them.

But instead she was stuck with this shorto king for who knew how long, watching him dancing around his roof—she caught another line and had to stop herself from clutching her breasts. What did he mean by all this? What was he getting at? She had worshipped at the temple of Ashtoreth often enough to get what he was saying, but "thigh joints"? Was he serious? And how long was this supposed to take? She looked critically at his fat knees, bouncing against the fabric of his new Oscan robe. She doubted *he* would be much good at holding her close, keeping her safe in the hold of a leaky boat as the waves roiled them about.

"Thy navel is like a round goblet which wasteth not liquor! Um, something about wheat. Breasts like clusters on the vine! Your nose smells like apples! Your—"

"Wait—what?"

"Um, your—your nose smells like apples?"

"Apples?"

"Don't you like apples?"

"Apples?"

"You don't like apples. I'll have Meshulle make a note of it. So, mmm, your nose is like . . . olive oil . . . and . . . "

"Olive oil?"

"You don't like olive oil either?" Incredible! Not even smeared on a bit of bread? No?"

The girl shook her head. She was certainly a strange one. Your average girl would be falling all over him by now: "Sup from my navel!" and so on. Curious. Could she be of Enheduanna's persuasion? Solomon had always wanted to meet one of those.

Solomon leaned to one side to catch the silhouette of her young breasts again, the slope of her legs. Nothing like an hourglass to focus the mind, he always said. Never failed to crack the boys up. He needed to remember to add that one to his book of wisdom.

"So what about me, eh?" Solomon patted his paunch. "Belly of bright ivory? Legs like pillars of marble?" He winked. "What about my mouth?"

He leaned forward and upward and Caíla leaned back and away, grimacing. "Please," she said.

Solomon opened his eyes and laughed. "I know what you mean. Shall we go get everything taken care of?"

"What?"

"Get married!"

"Married? Bu—"

"Sure, sure. Probably should just do it now, after all, get it done early, before lunch. I'm supposed to go check out the army or something this afternoon, but don't worry, I'll be with you tonight, make it official. Do you have a favo—oh! Silly me! Your father said you were a virgin. Usually the poor ones aren't, you know."

"Right . . . A virgin . . . " That was true enough. Cousins don't count.

The king held out his arm to her and she looked at it. "Shall we go?"

"Um . . . "

"You must be feeling like the luckiest girl in the world, eh? Marrying the famous King Solomon?"

"But— I— Actually—"

"'Actually'?"

"My father said—"

"Oh yes, he was quite pleased, wasn't he? Proud little man, your father."

"But the swatches—"

"Heh heh. All business. I appreciate that in a wife. Or a concubine, as in your case. But today is about love, my dear. Nothing more."

"But I— I— I'm still kind of young and— and I—"

"Young? How old are you?"

"I'm fifteen."

"I knew it!" He looked pleased with himself and rubbed his chest. "Fifteen's not so young, my dear. I've plenty of wives much younger than that."

"Right, but, ah, we Oscans don't usually— My father said—"

But he was off again: "I would drink the juice of thy pomegranate! My left hand under your head! My right hand entering your—"

Caíla's head jerked. She had never heard that word before but she was no prude; she could figure things out. Maybe she'd never actually *participated* in the goddess's rituals, but she had observed them often enough—and maybe all her experience had been in the dark, alone, without candles, trying to be quiet, giggling, whispering, but she was no fool. And no one had ever said anything like that to her before. She couldn't breathe.

"Oh. My. Gods."

"Ah-ah-ah! None of that pagan talk here! Didn't you know? My palace is dedicated to the Most High God."

"It is?"

"Certainly! Why, this garden is every bit as holy as the temple itself!"

"But I thought—"

"Oh, come now! You must know the story? How, when I first became king—I was all alone—and there was this light— and then the voice of God—"

"Omigods—you *are* serious. My father said no one believed that story, but you do. You totally do. I thought—I thought that—with the One God—because I saw those gods—in the courtyard—and that one—by the red flower—and I heard—at the temple—"

Solomon grimaced. He was used to this coming from his foreign queens—Pharaolina was still particularly awful (like having a hippo-headed goddess staring down at them from above the bed wasn't bad enough)—but this girl! This girl lived within his own city! How could this happen?

Of course, a quick glance at her tits convinced him it wasn't worth killing her over—that and the need for new draperies of course—but another unbeliever in the family! Ahimaaz would never let him hear the end of it.

"Can I go now?"

Solomon stared at her. He blinked. When his thoughts began again, they rummaged through his memory, searching for the last time someone—anyone!—had said that to him.

They found nothing.

"What."

She looked shorter now, shrunken. Her eyes wide, frightened. He bared his teeth and she fell to her knees. Finally. She saw him as a king.

"What did you say."

"Can—can I—go now—please?"

He pulled on her arm and dragged her until she stumbled to her feet. He yanked her to the stairwell, thrusting her ahead of him. "Birsha!" he screamed. "Birsha!!!"

Birsha scurried up the stairs, panting. "Yes m'liege?"

"Get a priest. We'll wed her now. Then take her to the harem and prepare her for tonight. Have the other concubines watch—the youngest ones—then get Reho-

boam. Tell him to deal with this one. He's always getting into the harem anyway, he may as well do something useful. Tell him she's too tall." Solomon paused a moment and accidentally smiled. Rehoboam was a good boy. Make a fine king some day. But, gods willing—er—God willing, he would never have so many wives. Solomon grimaced. Life had been so much pleasanter back when he'd only had seven hundred or so. If only they would stop getting older.

Solomon glared back at Caíla—her scared face, so pale and lovely; her breasts—it was as if he'd already seen them—

He had to have her, that much was simple.

The wedding was brief, but beautiful. The wives present cried.

Solomon went off to inspect, not the armies, but improvements to the city walls.

He came home that evening and went straight to the harem. On silk cushions lay Caíla, her legs and belly and breasts moist with oil, her eyes and cheeks with tears. Solomon removed his sweaty robes and tossed them to a young girl—maybe nine or ten—Solomon hadn't wanted her, but she'd come with her sister and a novelty's a novelty. Always nice to break up the routine.

Solomon walked over for a closer inspection, moving folds of skin, pinching lines onto her young breasts. If she wanted a god, he would show her a god. He was Solomon.

"Set me as a seal upon thine heart, for love is strong as death, jealousy is as cruel as the grave, the coals thereof are coals of fire, which burn with a most vehement flame."

Solomon smiled and settled down to his kingly duty.

Caíla lay on her back, thrust by waves no one would save her from.

HE WRONGED THE PEOPLE OF ISRAEL BY SAYING THINGS . . .

My father made your yoke heavy, and I will add to your yoke: my father also chastised you with whips, but I will chastise you with scorpions.

How to Get Over It

a public service message

The Rehoboam Method.

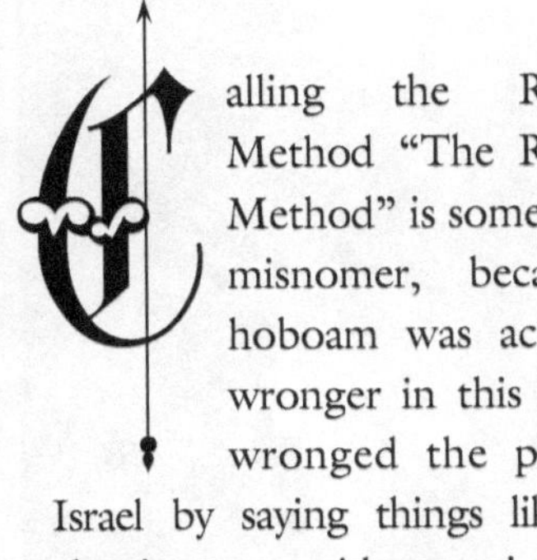

alling the Rehoboam Method "The Rehoboam Method" is something of a misnomer, because Rehoboam was actually the wronger in this story. He wronged the people of Israel by saying things like "I will chastise you with scorpions" when they hadn't even done anything that required chastising with lollipops. Rehoboam was, to be technical, a "punk."

What is instructive in this story is how the people of Israel Got Over It. The Bible simply reads that "all Israel went to their tents." In other words, get out of the situation, go home, do your own thing and, thus, Get Over It. A nice little method, that.

So Naaman did it, was cleaned, and praised God.

And his servants came near, and spake unto him, and said, My father, if the prophet had bid thee do some great thing, wouldest thou not have done it? how much rather then, when he saith to thee, Wash, and be clean?

How to Get Over It

a public service message

The Naaman Method.

Naaman, if you will recall, was a Syrian (of all things), and a highfalutin' Syrian at that. A highfalutin' Syrian with leprosy, that is. But he had heard about a prophet in Israel, a worker of miracles, and decided to come and get himself a miracle. When he arrived, the prophet didn't even bother to come out and see the highfalutin' Syrian with leprosy, but just sent out a messenger. And then—get this—the best this "prophet" could come up with was "Go and wash in Jordan seven times." Needless to say, Naaman was gravely insulted. First slighted, then insulted. He left in a huff. (As opposed to leaving in a minute and a huff.)

Fortunately, Naaman traveled about with a servant not so highfalutin' as himself who said, in essence. "Golly gee whiz, Naaman, sir, but it wouldn't *kill* you." So Naaman did it, was cleaned, and praised God.

The Naaman Method, then is to realize you're really blowing this whole thing out of proportion so just Get Over It already!

. . . I HAVE / NOTHING LEFT, UNLESS YOU TAKE / THE PALM OF THIS HAND.

The Palms of Her Hands

I name each finger

and still you are
unnamable.

Pointer: the call to a window,
your face appearing.

Middle: opposition in no things,
except the thumb reaching.

Ring: I am Jezebel,
before the dogs.

Little: so fragile, I have
nothing left, unless you take

the palm of this hand.

WHAT'S THAT? COME AGAIN? I CAN'T HEAR YOU.

From the Desk of Baal's Secretary

Hello? Yes, hello? No—I'm sorry:
I'm afraid Mr. Baal is not here.
An emergency? From where are you calling?
Out near Mt. Carmel? Well, I fear
Mr. Baal is engaged and he can't get away
from all of his business at hand.
It's a lot of work—well, *you* try being
the recognized god of the land.

What's that? Come again? I can't hear you.
You say you've constructed a pyre
and you're hoping that Baal will light it
with some of his patented fire?
Well, to process your order you'll need first
a pyrotechnician's permission.
One second, I'll transfer your call to
our fireball service division.

You don't want the transfer, you tell me?
It's Baal himself, or else naught?
Honey, believe me, a transfer
is all of the help that I've got.
I'm not going to break up Baal's meeting
to ask for a measly eruption.
You don't know, as I do, what he does
to the ones who create interruption.

Don't scream at me. Carmel's *your* problem;
Mr. Baal can't be used as a shield.
We don't have time or the money to float
representatives out in the field.
But there's competition there in your city
who can deliver them fire, you say?
Well, perhaps you should use *their* suppliers
and not bother me with your whining. Good *day!*

. . . WE SHOULD BE ABLE TO GET THE WALLS AROUND THE HOLY OF HOLIES . . .

Ye see the distress that we are in, how Jerusalem lieth waste, and the gates thereof are burned with fire: come, and let us build up the wall of Jerusalem, that we be no more a reproach.

Ezra's Inbox

From: zechariah@jew.judah.prs
To: ezra@temple.judah.prs, nehemiah@governor.judah.prs
Subject: New Prophet

The Lord has seen fit to send a second prophet to support us in telling the people of Israel to repent and to rebuild the city walls and the temple. I'm quite glad. I've been running short on metaphors.

I gave him your addresses. I'm sure he'll be contacting you soon. I think you'll like him.

Z

———————————————————

From: nehemiah@governor.judah.prs
To: ezra@temple.judah.prs
Subject: Re: New Prophet

Ezra,

I'm distressed that our progress is so slow that the Lord has seen fit to send us a second prophet. For the extra communication I am of course grateful, but the obvious reason for such communication is distressing.

I've been trying to do what we talked about, teach everyone about the flight from Egypt and how nothing is impossible with God and so forth, but it's slow going. The poverty in the city is terrible.

Which reminds me. I've heard a rumor that one of the temple priests has been offering to sell some of the vessels Artaxerxes just sent back. Check and make sure they were all catalogued, then see if you can run down the rumor. Hopefully it's not true. If you need any help, let me know.

Have you written Sanballat back lately? I haven't been. He doesn't understand 'no' so I'm hoping ignoring him will have an effect.

Keep the Faith,
Nehemiah

From: jeshua@temple.judah.prs
To: ezra@temple.judah.prs
Subject: Re: Newly Sent Vessels

I've heard the rumor too. Priest in question is Manasseh. I'll send him in to see you.

--j

From: nehemiah@governor.judah.prs
To: ezra@temple.judah.prs
Subject: Haggai

I heard you met him. How did it go?

From: nehemiah@governor.judah.prs
To: ezra@temple.judah.prs
Subject: Fwd: Fine. Be that way.

Thought you should know.

Keep the Faith,
Nehemiah

From: sanballat@governor.samaria.prs
To: nehemiah@governor.judah.prs
Subject: Fine. Be that way.

Nehemiah you simpleton, I don't get you. We have the same fathers! We worship the same God! Plus, you Jews are so poor you have to wipe your butts with dirt! How do you plan on building a temple? You're not Solomon! I'm way more Solomon than you are! But fine! Be that way! Just because Cyrus gave you Jerusalem doesn't mean you deserve it. I don't care what Isaiah said, he was still a pagan. Not like me and you. We're God's chosen. And the temple belongs to me as much as you.

This isn't over.

Negotiations will continue.

PS: Tobiah and I would love to meet you somewhere for dinner some time, either here in Samaria or over in Ammon. We would be happy to put you up.

King Sanballat
Governor of Samaria
Vassal of the Great Artaxerxes

From: haggai@jew.judah.prs
To: nehemiah@governor.judah.prs, ezra@temple.judah.prs, zechariah@jew.judah.prs
Subject: Consider your ways!

You have sown much yet bring in little; you beat but don't have enough; you drink but are not filled; you clothe yourselves but none are warm.

He that earns wages earns wages just to put it in a bag with holes.

Thus saith the Lord of Hosts: Consider your ways!

From: haggai@jew.judah.prs
To: ezra@temple.judah.prs
Subject: Re: Consider your ways!

Thanks. It was nice to meet you too.

Consider your ways!

From: zechariah@jew.judah.prs
To: ezra@temple.judah.prs, nehemiah@governor.judah.prs
Subject: Vision of Horses

I have dreamed a dream and in my dream I did see horses, five of them.

A man was riding upon the red horse, and he stood among the myrtle trees and behind him were red, white and sort of russet horses.

So I asked, Lord, what are these? And an angel talked with me and said, I'll show you what these are.

And the guy on the red horse said, These are who the Lord's sent to walk to and fro through the earth.

And then the angel said, O Lord, how long will you not have mercy on Jerusalem and on the cities of Judah?

And the Lord answered the angel with good words and comfortable words.

So the angel said to me, Cry out, saying, Thus saith the Lord of hosts: I am jealous for Jerusalem and for Zion. And I am pretty upset with the heathen that are just lazing around.

But! Thus saith the Lord: I have returned to Jerusalem in mercy and my house will be built.

Z

PS: I'm going to be wandering in the wilderness the next couple weeks. Haggai should be able to handle any prophet stuff while I'm gone.

From: nehemiah@governor.judah.prs
To: ezra@temple.judah.prs
Subject: Arms

I've armed the men working on the wall. It's becoming apparent that these aren't random Samaritans, Sanballat's behind this. I can tell by his snide tone. Not that it's at all surprising.

Here's a bit from his latest message:

You know of course that I couldn't possibly have anything at all to do with such horrible happenings. You know I know how excellent the rebuilding of the City of Peace is. Lucky you to be God's chosen people. Wooooo.

Keep the Faith,
Nehemiah

From: jeshua@temple.judah.prs
To: ezra@temple.judah.prs
Subject: Manasseh

Have you heard about Manasseh? I'll come up this afternoon to tell you more about it.

Also, thanks for the vision from Zechariah. It was nice to hear something positive. If you see him before he leaves, ask him if he has time to talk to me about it.

Thanks.

From: manasseh@temple.judah.prs
To: ezra@temple.judah.prs
Subject: Wife

I've been thinking about what you said and I've decided that the Lord can't possibly mean that. I know you've been telling everyone that for years now and I supposed it makes sense for regular people, but as fellow priests, we should make an exception. Especially since she's a king's daughter. I'll be able to help smooth things over with the Samaritans. It would be so helpful to have them in bed with us, so to speak. I've been talking with Sanballat a lot lately and he's not as bad as everyone says. Did you know he wants to help build the temple but Nehemiah won't let him? That's gotta be the stupidest thing I've ever heard. We shouldn't be letting that Persian run things anyway. He doesn't have any priestly blood—you and I should be running the rebuilding.

Anyway, I'm going to bring my wife around so you can meet her and we can talk about getting Sanballat's help with the temple. I've already sent him some stuff on the priesthood so he can get something more legitimate set up over there. Of course, we don't want them to actually have the priesthood, but they need to know that God gave it to us. They seem to respect that.

I'll probably come by tomorrow morning.

-----Manasseh.

From: manasseh@temple.judah.prs
To: ezra@temple.judah.prs
Subject: Re: Wife

Where do you get off telling me what the Lord wants? I have just as much priesthood as you. It's not like you're a prophet either. I'm not even sure we have any prophets at the moment. You don't want to see my wife, okay. Your loss. If you knew what she was like you wouldn't want to spend any more nights with that hag Jewess anymore. Samaria is full of stuff you don't know anything about. You sit there with your big plans and your puppet ears and your doomsaying prophets and claim to know what's going on. Well you don't.

From: manasseh@temple.judah.prs
To: ezra@temple.judah.prs
Subject: Re: Wife

Don't try to be nice to me you blasphemer. I don't have to put up with this. My friends are kings. You wouldn't know a king if he spit in your eye.

Don't bother replying. I'm leaving. Consider my temple account canceled.

From: nehemiah@governor.judah.prs
To: ezra@temple.judah.prs
Subject: Re: Manasseh

I found some people who may have seen them, but nothing for sure. Anyway, he's gone now. I imagine to her father's house.

Keep the Faith,
Nehemiah

From: haggai@jew.judah.prs
To: nehemiah@governor.judah.prs, ezra@temple.judah.prs
Subject: Re: Delays

For behold, the daily problems of building are a direct result of the wickedness of Judah! The Lord will not sustain us so long as we love our own lives more than his glory!

Consider your ways!

A little while and I will shake the heavens! and the earth! and the sea! and the dry land! and all the nations! and I will fill this house with glory, saith the Lord of hosts.

From: nehemiah@governor.judah.prs
To: ezra@temple.judah.prs
Cc: zechariah@jew.judah.prs, haggai@jew.judah.prs
Subject: Re: Temple update, etc.

The wall is coming along excellent, thank you for asking. You need to come out to the east side—you won't recognize it.

As for the temple, I wrote Artaxerxes earlier today to let him know we completed the safehold for the new vessels, but while I was inspecting it I noticed that things are in disarray. I talked to Jeshua about it, but he seemed surprised. For safety's sake I've armed the workers on the temple as well. I'm speaking outside the temple tonight to the people about the need to stand strong and protect ourselves, to not be afraid of those against us, but to remember the Lord who is great and terrible, and to fight for our brethren, our sons, and our daughters, our wives, and our houses. Something like that. How the Lord won't save us till we demonstrate our worth and seriousness to the cause. It would be great if you could come and talk as well. (This invite's also open to you, Zechariah and Haggai. As Zechariah was telling me yesterday, the Lord's still disappointed with our progress, progressing though it may be.)

On the bright side, we finally got the pulley system working for the temple's inner walls. If it holds strong, we should be able to get the walls around the Holy of Holies up before the new year.

Sanballat wrote me earlier today, gloating about Manasseh. I think we need to seriously consider the possibility of increased hostility from Samaria, and possibly Ammon. Your prayers sustain the men on the walls, but any additional token of gratitude would go a long way for morale.

Keep the Faith,
Nehemiah

From: artaxerxes@shah.prs
To: nehemiah@governor.judah.prs, ezra@temple.judah.prs
Subject: How's my favorite Jews?

Nehemiah! Ezra! How's the "Promised Land"? I've been going over some more records with the treasury and I think we've finally sent back all the stuff for the temple.* Tell your One God that Cyrus's heirs have fulfilled the prophecy. Also, I'm setting up a lottery to determine what other Jews to send back. What do you think—a couple thousand families a year too much?

(*Unless: did you guys have any golden breasts? No one's sure where they came from. They don't really seem your style, but if they are yours let me know. Otherwise, I'm totally putting them in the eunuchs' chambers. Maybe it's just me, but the idea cracks me up.)

Nehemiah—Damaspia told me to tell you she's moving out of your old place. I told her you wouldn't be interested, but she made me promise to tell you. She feels terrible. You might drop her a line—it's damaspia@queens.shah.prs. Thanks.

The other vassal states I set up like yours aren't really taking. Most people don't ever remember who they used to be. Not that I blame them. It's pretty great to be Persian. Either of you guys decide to come back, I've got plenty for you to do here.

We have elephants in the capital this week. I'm trying to get a breeding program going. If it works, you want any?

Anyway, I'm rambling. I'll have my people get you details if you're interested.

Tell Rachel hi for me, Nemmy.

Keep up the good work, Ezra.

Artaxerxes
Great Shah of Persia
Pharaoh of Egypt
Heir of Cyrus
Emperor Achaemenid

From: zechariah@jew.judah.prs
To: ezra@temple.judah.prs
Subject: Armageddon

Thank you for dinner last night. My family had been fasting with me so I apologize if the boys seemed a little overeager. It's been hard on them with their mother running the sewing detail. Which reminds me . . . When you see Nehemiah this afternoon, tell him to send someone over. The new trousers for the wall-builders are ready. I forgot to tell him earlier and I'm sure you'll see him before he could get a message from me. Besides, I should already be out on the street warning the citizenry.

I'll be talking some more about Armageddon, but I've been receiving some happier stuff lately as well. Haggai's planning on being at the temple tonight, so I'll have him drop off a copy of my notes. There's this great thing about our sins being carted away to Babylon—it's really great. I hope I'll be able to share it with everyone soon. But tonight's mostly a reprise of "Jerusalem is a burdensome stone" with more details of disaster. It's what the people need.

It would be great if you could talk to Jeshua about the filthiness of his garments again.

As for you, you're to study the four horns more deeply. If you have any questions, let me know.

Z

From: sanballat@governor.samaria.prs
To: ezra@temple.judah.prs
Subject: Nehemiah

Ezra. You're a reasonable man. Manasseh speaks very highly of you—like a father you were to him. Walk yourself over to Nehemiah and tell him I am not your enemy. We do worship the same God, after all.

Anyway, I'm putting Manasseh in your position. Nothing personal of course, and if you help me out I certainly won't get rid of you, but Nehemiah and that Jeshua person are as good as gone already. I wouldn't stand too close if you know what I mean.

Consider your position well.

King Sanballat
Persia & Samaria

PS: Next time you see Nehemiah, tell him I'm having Tobiah over next week and we would love to meet with him to talk about the rain situation. Nothing official, just an informal meeting of governors.

From: noadiah@jew.judah.prs
To: ezra@temple.judah.prs, nehemiah@governor.judah.prs
Subject: Wickedness of Israel

Thus sayeth the Lord God unto my prophetess Noadiah: the people are wrapt in gross wickedness, listening to false prophets and following blind leaders, building walls where no walls need be built, trusting in their own flesh rather than the hand of God to deliver them! Thus saith the Lord: if my people would be free of Persia, instead of listening to the friends of Persia they would give of their wealth unto the poor of spirit and the holy of God for distribution to the chosen vessels of the Lord.

Let it so be written in your hearts.

From: nehemiah@governor.judah.prs
To: ezra@temple.judah.prs, zechariah@jew.judah.prs, haggai@jew.judah.prs, jeshua@temple.judah.prs
Subject: Who is Noadiah?

Anyone know who she is? A lot of the workers have been to hear her preach, but I don't know anything.

Keep the Faith,
Nehemiah

From: zechariah@jew.judah.prs
To: nehemiah@governor.judah.prs, ezra@temple.judah.prs, haggai@jew.judah.prs, jeshua@temple.judah.prs
Subject: Re: Who is Noadiah?

She is not of God.

From: haggai@jew.judah.prs
To: nehemiah@governor.judah.prs, ezra@temple.judah.prs, zechariah@jew.judah.prs, jeshua@temple.judah.prs
Subject: Re: Who is Noadiah?

The latter house shall be greater than the first and that final temple shall not come without much suffering and tribulation upon the people of God.

Consider your ways!

From: jeshua@temple.judah.prs
To: ezra@temple.judah.prs
Subject: False prophets

Do we have a policy in place to deal with the preaching of false prophets upon temple grounds? They're becoming oppressive.

--j

From: manasseh@gerizim.samaria.prs
To: ezra@temple.judah.prs
Subject: Feast of Tabernacles

I'm putting together a group of believers to bring over for the feast of tabernacles. I know you'll need me to help with the translation because Jeshua is just terrible at it. Also, it would be great if you would let us do some sacrifices before the regular stuff gets started. Sanballat, holy be his name, has given us animals for the Lord.

See you soon,

-----Manasseh.

From: manasseh@gerizim.samaria.prs
To: ezra@temple.judah.prs
Subject: Re: Feast of Tabernacles

I don't see how that's any of your blaspheming business.

From: nehemiah@governor.judah.prs
To: ezra@temple.judah.prs
Subject: Re: Fwd: Feast of Tabernacles

I'll move some more men to the walls, just to be safe. May I suggest the priests put the heat back on the heathen-wives issue? That's what got us into this mess in the first place after all, and I really don't think we've made much progress.

Keep the Faith,
Nehemiah

From: artaxerxes@shah.prs
To: ezra@temple.judah.prs
Subject: Re: Happy Birthday

Thanks, Ez. Very funny. I can see why Nemmy likes you so much. I wish I could come and see what you two are accomplishing out there.

Keep up the good work.

Artaxerxes
Great Shah of Persia
Pharaoh of Egypt
Heir of Cyrus
Emperor Achaemenid

From: zechariah@jew.judah.prs
To: ezra@temple.judah.prs, nehemiah@governor.judah.prs
Subject: Message from the Lord

Deliver yourself, O Zion, from dwelling with the fallen daughters of the world—
for they that touch you touch the apple of my eye and I will shake my hand
upon them and you shall know that the Lord of hosts has done it.

Sing and rejoice, O daughter of Zion: for I come and will dwell with you.

And many nations will be joined to me in that day and shall be my people, and
I will dwell amongst you.

And the Lord shall inherit Judah, and shall choose Jerusalem again.

From: nehemiah@governor.judah.prs
To: ezra@temple.judah.prs
Subject: Fwd: Nothing left to do but tell the truth

Of course, I'm quaking in my sandals.

From: sanballat@governor.samaria.prs
To: nehemiah@governor.judah.prs
Subject: Nothing left to do but tell the truth

I've tried reasoning with you. I've invited you over for boar and even for that bat soup you Persians are supposed to like so much which you must not realize costs more than any Jew can afford, you Persian-born poser. You're no more a child of Abraham than the emperor. So there's nothing left to do but let him know that your stupid Jewish nation is in rebellion, attacking its loyal neighbors (me!) and cutting off trade from Egypt and glorifying a false version of the Lord God, valuing it greater than the glorious state of Persia, and not letting us, the loyal ones, use the temple.

You don't know what the emperor is like, but I do. You have no idea what men with true power are capable of.

You won't be governor long.

But fret not. I will let you lick my heels before I crush you with the full force of the Persian army.

Sanballat

From: haggai@jew.judah.prs
To: nehemiah@governor.judah.prs, ezra@temple.judah.prs, jeshua@temple.judah.prs, zechariah@jew.judah.prs
Subject: Bearers of holy flesh

Thus saith the Lord of hosts: If one bears holy flesh in the skirt of his garment and with his skirt touches bread or pottage or wine or oil or any meat, will it be holy? No.

If one that is unclean by a dead body touches any of these, shall it be unclean? It shall.

So is this people before me, saith the Lord. Every work of their hands which they offer is unclean.

Therefore I ask you to consider, from this day up, before even one temple stone was laid upon another, this: When one came to a heap of twenty measures, there were but ten; when one came to the pressfat to draw fifty vessels, there were but twenty. I smote you with blasting and with mildew and with hail yet you did not turn to me.

Consider now, from this day up, consider it.

Is seed yet in the barn? Yes. But the grapes and the figs and the pomegranates and the olives have not brought forth.

From this day forth will I bless you.

Consider your ways!

From: noadiah@jew.judah.prs
To: nehemiah@governor.judah.prs, ezra@temple.judah.prs
Subject: God's Temple

Remember it is the righteous the temple belongs to! Not the sinner! Abandon your offices before God smites you in his wrath!

From: nehemiah@governor.judah.prs
To: ezra@temple.judah.prs
Subject: Re: Bearers of holy flesh

You're a priest. Can you make anything of this?

From: zechariah@jew.judah.prs
To: ezra@temple.judah.prs
Subject: Re: Bearers of holy flesh

Kind of reminds you of that stuff my grandpa Iddo received, doesn't it? At least it's good news, right?

Anyway, here's the woman-in-the-ephah thing you wanted:

Then the angel said to me, "Lift up your eyes, and see what you see. " And I said, "What is it?" And he said, "It is an ephah with a woman sitting beside it and a talent of lead to put on top of it. This is wickedness." And the angel cast the woman into the ephah and the weight of lead upon its mouth.

Then I looked up and beheld that there came out two women and the wind was in their wings—for they had wings like the wings of a stork—and they took the ephah away. So I said to the angel, "Where are they taking it?" And he said, "To build a house for it far, far away. In Babylon it shall be established, and not here."

Z

From: nehemiah@governor.judah.prs
To: ezra@temple.judah.prs
Subject: Re: Bearers of holy flesh

Thanks. I liked the "From this day forth will I bless you" bit, but I didn't want to assume too much. I figured it could still be just another Repent! thing. Not to make light of it, of course. Do you know if Haggai has tried it out on the streets yet? Maybe it will work. It would be nice.

See you tomorrow.

Keep the Faith,
Nehemiah

From: manasseh@gerizim.samaria.prs
To: sanballat@governor.samaria.prs
Cc: holy_priests_of_samaria-list@gerizim.samaria.prs,
holy_fertility_guild-list@gerizim.samaria.prs,
admin-list@governor.samaria.prs, prophets_of_judah-list@judah.prs,
nehemiah@governor.judah.prs, ezra@temple.judah.prs,
zechariah@jew.judah.prs
Subject: Feast of the Holy Mountain

By revelation and under the auspices of Holy Vessel King Sanballat Governor of Samaria, Manasseh the high priest of Mount Gerizim the Holy Temple to the Lord announces the first holy Feast of the Holy Mountain at Mount Gerizim.

In commemoration of this blessed event, we will be making celebratory robes of palm fronds and myrtle and willow branches. This is a step up from just waving them around like the Jews do. We will also have lemonade. We're calling this opening ceremony the Samarikkot.

Here's what the schedule will look like:

<u>Sundown:</u> Samarikkot.

<u>That night:</u> Mostly drinking and getting to know each other better. The HFG is handling this.

<u>Sunrise:</u> In honor of the creation of the world and the deliverance of us from wickedness by Holy Sanballat, we will rest in tents at this point.

<u>Around noon:</u> The HFG has entertainment arranged for the remaining daylight hours.

<u>Sundown:</u> Samarikkot again, only by this time everyone should be in tune enough with eternity to not need the ceremonial lulav robes which, let's face it, probably won't be that comfortable anyway.

The next two days will proceed much the same. Just before sunrise on the third day, we'll light whatever robes are left on fire.

All the holy children of the God of Abraham are invited. Please make those you serve aware of the opportunities for worship that await them.

Remember that full observance of the Feast of the Holy Mountain is necessary for an adequate harvest.

When the Lord fills your cup, it spills over.

Manasseh
High Priest to the Most High God

From: noadiah@jew.judah.prs
To: manasseh@gerizim.samaria.prs
Cc: sanballat@governor.samaria.prs, admin-list@governor.samaria.prs, holy_priests_of_samaria-list@gerizim.samaria.prs, holy_fertility_guild-list@gerizim.samaria.prs, prophets_of_judah-list@judah.prs, nehemiah@governor.judah.prs, ezra@temple.judah.prs, zechariah@jew.judah.prs
Subject: Re: Feast of the Holy Mountain

Behold! Thus saith the Lord! Whosoever goeth to the Feast of the Holy Mountain shall perish! Thus saith the Lord!

From: nehemiah@governor.judah.prs
To: ezra@temple.judah.prs
Subject: Re: Feast of the Holy Mountain

Well, it looks like she got one right finally.

I ran into her earlier this afternoon and she's planning on going to Gerizim and preaching during the festivities. I would be glad to be rid of her, but I'm concerned she'll find a receptive audience for some of her other stuff—like tearing down the city walls. Thoughts?

Speaking of walls, we are going to have to go back to the quarry after all. I'm planning on leaving right after the Sabbath and should be back the next day, but the workers won't be back until they finish the job. I want to send a priest with them for Sabbath observance however long they're gone. If you and Jeshua could work that out and let me know, I would be grateful. I'll talk to you next time I'm at the temple.

How is the new guard situation working out? They aren't in your way, are they?

Keep the Faith,
Nehemiah

From: haggai@jew.judah.prs
To: nehemiah@governor.judah.prs, ezra@temple.judah.prs
Subject: Consider your ways!

Consider your ways!

From: nehemiah@governor.judah.prs
To: ezra@temple.judah.prs
Cc: zechariah@jew.judah.prs, haggai@jew.judah.prs
Subject: Sanballat

Artaxerxes has been getting mail from Sanballat about our "ever-increasing" disloyalty. He just sent me the latest version of Judah's Sins According to Sanballat and wants to know if he should dispose of him as governor. I'm leaning no—any replacement might be more competently harmful.

I plan on making this an issue of fasting and prayer. Your input is welcome.

Keep the Faith,
Nehemiah

From: zechariah@jew.judah.prs
To: ezra@temple.judah.prs
Cc: nehemiah@governor.judah.prs
Subject: Book

Jeshua's been helping me compile and organize my prophecies and he happened to mention that you two are also keeping records (as you should) and that Ezra, you've even finished a new history of Israel. Any chance I could come by and read what you have?

Thanks,

Z

From: nehemiah@governor.judah.prs
To: ezra@temple.judah.prs
Subject: Re: Book

Have you actually finished that history? I would love to read it if you have.

Keep the Faith,
Nehemiah

From: jeshua@temple.judah.prs
To: ezra@temple.judah.prs
Subject: Clean

Thank you for letting me come in last night. I can't believe the Lord is so patient with me.

--j

From: haggai@jew.judah.prs
To: nehemiah@governor.judah.prs, ezra@temple.judah.prs,
zechariah@jew.judah.prs, jeshua@temple.judah.prs
Subject: Temple

In a little while, God will shake his kingdoms and fill his house with Glory.

Consider your ways!

PS: Thanks for the figs

From: manasseh@gerizim.samaria.prs
To: ezra@temple.judah.prs
Subject: You

Thanks for nothing, you blasphemer. I'll have you know our crops are great this year. Who knows God now?

Lord Manasseh
The High Priest over Creation at Mount Gerizim

From: zechariah@jew.judah.prs
To: ezra@temple.judah.prs
Subject: Re: Some questions about yesterday's prophesying

No, the Lord's happy with the four festivals themselves, the problem is that no one remembers why we hold them.

We need the people to return to God—the whole purpose of the festivals is to remember how God brought us back here to this city, this land. Forgetting him again will just lead to our destruction again.

But you're not the one who needs to hear this. The Lord is pleased with you and the priests. But so many of us have clearly forgotten what they're all about.

I'm sure you are every bit as distressed as I am.

Jerusalem is now a fractured city without either young or old, but as they leave behind their idols and follow the true shepherd, they will become prisoners of hope and the Lord their God shall save them.

We will hear the laughter of small children. We will have the wisdom of ancients. The Lord loves his people and looks after us.

Holiness to the Lord.

As for Sanballat, the Lord has decreed that those who do not worship him shall receive no rain. I rather expect that applies to our brothers the Samaritans.

Before I go, I have a question about the law so I'll be coming by to see Jeshua later today. If you can, return from your meeting with Nehemiah a bit early so we can talk.

Thanks,

Z

From: nehemiah@governor.judah.prs
To: ezra@temple.judah.prs
Subject: Considering my ways

I met with Haggai about the building of the temple and I shared with him that notice from Artaxerxes that the vassal states are being cut a little looser and we agreed that the success we're receiving is remarkable. He explained that holy-flesh thing to me a little better and my impression really is that, overall, the Lord accepts our efforts.

I don't know how much we'll be able to accomplish before we die and I hope the Lord will let me stay and help out a long, long time. I think I could stay here forever so long as I have good men like you at my side.

Rachel's going to join us for lunch, then I think I may just go home—I haven't seen my children since the Sabbath.

Before the end of the week though, I need you to show me what needs to be prioritized on the temple project.

Thanks for everything you do, Ezra.

Keep the Faith,
Nehemiah

. . . TO HIM HER KITH AND / KIN CONFESSTHER.

And the king loved Esther above all the women, and she obtained grace and favour in his sight more than all the virgins; so that he set the royal crown upon her head, and made her queen . . .

The Queen Jew

Esther, Esther,
had a messther
tougher than a
game of chessther.
To the king she
had said yesther
she was now the
king's princessther.
(But oh, but oh, what could she do?
Esther, Esther, was a Jew!)

Esther, Esther's,
unc' expressther
things said in the
king's congressther:
Jews that were a
slight successther,
nobles wanted
to oppressther.
(Oppress here means "to have their head."
Esther, Esther, they wanted *dead.*)

Esther, Esther,
God would blessther.
So, she wore the
perfect dressther.
And, underneath the
king's caressther
to him her kith and
kin confessther.
(The law was changed throughout the city.
Esther, Esther, was quite pretty.)

Esther, Esther's
Jews progressther.
What will happen

Esther-lessther?
(We do not even
need to guessther.)

YOU'LL NEVER FIND MORE LOYAL FRIENDS . . .

And the Lord said unto Satan, Hast thou considered my servant Job, that there is none like him in the earth, a perfect and an upright man, one that feareth God, and escheweth evil?

The Love Song

OF

Eliphaz, Bildad, and Zophar

If you are sad, we'll come to you,
if you are sick, we'll bear you up,
if you have pain, we'll sit with you
and help you drink the bitter cup.

You'll never find more loyal friends,
not under heaven's arching vault!
In trio, we will pass the time
reminding you *it's all your fault.*

. . . Behira and I felt that Roniel stood apart from our family and she felt we shut her out.

The Book of Job's Wife

With my own hand I will write the names of my children, so that they will not be forgotten.

I am not a scribe. I am nothing more than the wife of a famous man, but I have learned to write and I know no one will record my children's names but me. The scribes who have written Job's story say there is not room to write them all; it is enough, they say, to know that he had many children before his troubles began. But to know the thing that befell my family one must know beginnings from endings, must know what we lost to learn what we gained in the end.

My husband Job was a great success; his fields were on level land near the streams, and each year the yield was larger. As the only son of his parents he inherited their lands, and his holdings increased with the dowry of my marriage. We had not been married long before he turned his wealth to trading: Uz was gaining importance as a stop on the way to Egypt that avoided the war-ravaged lands to the west, and Job was first to set up a trading post and then, four years later, began to send his own caravans. Our wealth grew greater as our family grew.

I had five children. My daughter Naomi, so solemn from childhood to adulthood, who grew like the tree of a rich woman's garden, straight and slim. She made a good marriage and showed a quiet happiness. My son Idan, furious in the world of ideas, who spoke loudly to the rafters of the ceiling when the mood of declaiming took him until they shook, who envied the Levites their place in the priesthood. My second son Moshe, soft-spoken and careful in everything he said, who could make even Job listen to him when his sentences ran three or more at a time. And then wild Zafrir, with his ready smile, and Dor, the son of my consolation in my old age, with his goat's voice and his jokes.

There were others in our household; as befitted his station, Job had three wives of the surrounding towns. Behira was his second wife, grown like a sister to me in the many years we had shared our home, her children like my own—rosy Margalit, the cheerfully squabbling sons Alon and Harel, and everyone's darling, the curly-headed Kochaua. And there was of course Roniel, Job's third wife of but ten years, whose son Gidon played with the children of my children as if they were his brothers and sisters.

At this end of my troubles it is easy to say our hearts were never darkened in those days, but it is not so. We had our trials, like any family—our children fought, Job and his sons argued about God's law, Behira and I felt that Roniel stood apart from our family and she felt we shut her out. But we were happy in those days, and monthly sent the thanks-offerings to show our gratitude for our lot.

"Success begets success," Job would often say in those days. "Good actions bring good." He had given overgenerously to the merchant Calev to feed his family, and Behira had asked him if it were wise. His arm about her, he said, "What good we do finds its way back to us, no matter how long it takes to travel."

"Calev is a good investment," said Roniel, at the bread-board. She and Calev were related, distantly. "He looks to be a successful merchant."

"You would want to gift Calev until he competes with you," said Behira to Job, laughing. Her laugh was like a bird's; she sang often in those days in a light and clear voice.

"If it is God's will," said Job, but we all knew that he did not think that it was.

Our children grew up and out of our house—Job set up an outpost in Shuhua and my sons moved there, and it seemed as if our riches doubled overnight. I began to be invited to the homes of the richest women in Uz. On the day that Elseba, the wife of our judge, sent her messengers to us I knew that we had become very rich, indeed. And it was not many years before it was my duty to invite Elseba to our home, as we had grown even more blessed. And though she sniffed at the simplicity of our rooms, I know she left impressed. We were important in the sight of the people of Uz, and none more important than Job.

The day that our troubles befell us came the year after our greatest harvest. Job had begun to speak of building an outpost in Beth-channan, where Behira had been born, and Moshe, Zafrir, and Alon had spent the summer season there, to see what traffic traveled there toward

Egypt. We planned a great feast to welcome them at Idan's home in Shuhua. We were to be there for their arrival and spend a fortnight together as a family.

On the tiniest things does the fate of our lives rest. Roniel developed a tiny cough on the day before our departure, and as it was the season of disease we felt it best to stay behind while our children went on, hale and hearty, to the feasting.

"We will join you in a day's time," said Job, laughing, as he embraced Gidon—now grown almost to a man. "It will be good for the children to abuse their parents for an evening before Papa comes and ruins the fun."

"As long as Papa pays for the feast!" laughed Gidon, as he leapt upon the wain already carrying his brothers and sisters, and many of their children. It has haunted me since that we did not watch the wagon leave. It seemed such a small thing—another coming and going in a busy life—but it was the last time I saw those children on this world.

"It will be rest, without chattering children," said Job at the meal that night, but he didn't mean it, for he asked Roniel three times if she felt well enough that we could leave in the morning.

But we would not leave the next morning. If we had, we may have witnessed our desolation first-hand.

It was not until noon of the next day that Roniel announced that she felt well enough to travel. We had just begun to pack for our journey—joking among ourselves as we did when we worked together—when there was a shout at the gate and then, before any of us could move to the door, three servants from our lands in Shuhua burst into our main doors, beside themselves with a panicked exhaustion.

I do not know why it has worried me so since, but I am bothered that I never knew their names, these faithful servants who changed our lives with a few simple words. They were able-looking men, all young, for they had run from Shuhua, which was a few leagues hence. They were weeping, which showed their loyalty, and they spoke all at once, confusedly, in the tones of disaster.

We watched them, frozen. I had a folded blanket in my hands—I can still feel its rough threads in the force of my grip.

"Speak clearly," said Job in a bark, and though it seemed to me too sharp it had its effect, the young men swallowed their babble and the one standing nearest me said, "My lord Job, there has been a terrible fire. Your children—your children are dead."

There are some things that are greater than the words we have to describe them. I cannot hope to explain the horror of that moment. The three of us stood as if struck into stone. For a swift, wild moment I thought I would laugh, as if laughter would turn the moment into some perverse joke.

"Dead?" said Job, even sterner than before.

Another youth swallowed and spoke, even as he still wept. "None in the house survived, Lord. There—there was lightning, lightning but no rain, and the house was still thatched—" We had planned to build with stone after the profits of the year's harvest: the winters had been mild in Shuhua.

"None? Not one survived?" Job was close to roaring.

The youths looked among themselves and could not speak. It was answer enough.

A number of things happened at once. I dropped my blanket and Job reached across and gripped my hand so hard that it hurt. Behira said, "Oh—" very softly into the silence. And, after a moment, Roniel fell to her knees from the cushion she had been sitting on and began to scream with sobs.

It was the single moment of my life, the most enormous, and it left me breathless. I felt the stupidity of a dream settle upon me and all I did. And yet there was much to do. Job said that we must go to Shuhua at once, and that we must take a priest

in case it were true, and when he said that, neither Behira nor Roniel would allow themselves to be left behind in the empty house. And so we had to pack as if nothing had happened, but quickly, as Job wished to leave at once. There was food to think of, and comfort for Roniel, and there was no help from Job, as he had gone to send swift messengers to check the truth of the youths' story.

It was a nightmare journey, though the road to Shuhua is not long in a cart. I think we all hoped that there had been some ghastly mistake, but at each leg of our journey the messengers Job had sent returned to us, relaying not just the truth of the fire but further misfortunes: the lack of a master in the outpost had left the stables and granaries free to marauders, and they had been despoiled. The sheep flocks had escaped their fire-ravaged paddocks and had escaped to the hills. The market-post we had set up so carefully had been pulled down and plucked of its merchandise. There seemed no end to the terrors that awaited us in Shuhua, but our thoughts still centered around our children. It seemed impossible that all of them would have been struck down.

But when we arrived at our holdings in Shuhua, we saw at once that there could have been no survivors.

The house and land had been blasted by fire: not one thing remained. Standing in front of our desolation, I held Behira who found it hard to stand, while Job held the weeping Roniel. Our fortunes were gone, our family had been destroyed, almost erased, and there were only the four of us, three old women and one old man, staring at the end of the world.

I felt then that I would collapse and die, that the earth I stood on would swallow me up in the pain that I was feeling. It was as if some creature of the desert suddenly sank its great talons into my heart and was intent upon tearing me to shreds. But with the weight of Behira sagging upon me and the pain of Job's helpless blue eyes staring across his ravaged futures, I knew I could not come apart under the onslaught of the thing attacking me. And so I drew Behira closer to me and began to plan, in a halting way, what things needed to happen next. There would be a funeral, of course, and the sacrifices which needed to be made, and we would have to release the servants we kept in Shuhua or bring them to our home in Uz. With these thoughts, my grief receded somewhat, and though I wept I did not bend my back in misery.

It was a trick that I learned in the days and nights that followed. If there were things to do, I could do them slowly one at a time, and my horrible grief would stay a step away from overtaking me. And there were many things to do, things that Behira and Roniel and even Job were too grief-wracked to perform. I found us lodging until the funeral. I organized the feasts. I bought the oxen for sacrifice. And ever I looked for something more to do.

"Hadasa, you are so brave," said Behira one night as we slept in the inn at Shuhua, the night before the funeral. "I don't know how you have done all that you have done this week."

"It isn't bravery," I said. "It's cowardice. I don't know what would happen if I stop." And at that I wept, and Behira sat with me with her head upon my shoulder.

The funeral was well-attended, for our children had been popular in Shuhua. As a courtesy, our friends from Uz traveled there, and there were many of the nobles from the surrounding cities who made the trip or sent messages of bereavement. We stood apart from them, as four mourners, in our garb and making the noises of sorrow, none so much as Roniel, who screamed out her sorrow to the heavens.

"She is inconsolable," said Job to me, once again his hand in mine, and said it to the crowd when they looked Roniel's way; perhaps he said it to the heavens as well. I have thought since then that he may have envied her and her vocal hurt.

The priest whom we had called to perform the rites attempted to comfort her. "God has called them home," he said.

"God!" cried Roniel, her voice shrill. "What does God know of this? This is nothing of God. God has abandoned us."

"Roniel—" began Behira, and even in the muteness of my grief I saw how beautiful she was, a woman in sorrow, her hands out to comfort Roniel even though the tears flowed freely down her ashen face.

"Don't touch me!" shrieked Roniel, flinching away from Behira, from the crowd, from the world. "What good are prayers and sacrifices? Why do we seek to protect ourselves? We are alone, alone—"

Job clutched my hand harder, but we could not bestir ourselves. The grief was a heavy stone upon us. I have thought—then and since— how remarkable it was that even in my mourning I avoided the grief that beset me. It felt at times that I watched myself at a great distance, and that I grieved almost without caring. At times it seemed I saw myself do the work of a mourner; at times the grieving exhausted me.

We felt that there could be no greater blow, to lose so greatly in so short a time. Behira and I wept much, quietly, in our moments.

Roniel, after her display at the funeral, spent her days in her chambers, screaming at God. We tried to comfort her, but she ran us from the room.

"What will we do?" I asked Behira as we made the common meal.

"She is younger than we are," said Behira quietly, kneading the bread. "She will mend in time."

Job turned to work to bear his sorrow, hoping to remake his fortunes. He spent his days haggling with the merchants to find some value in our remaining holdings. It was too late to plant another crop, and Job was eventually forced to sell our possessions, bit by bit.

"We will gain it back next year, after the harvests," he said heavily one day after he had sold most of our great oil urns. "With our remaining lands, we will make enough to return us to comfort."

"There is little comfort left," I said. It was a dark time for me, and I spent much of it in a stunned and sorry confusion.

He nodded into his beard, exhausted. "God will provide."

"What does it profit us, if God takes away everything he provides?"

He had no answer for that, so he took me into his arms and let me cry.

But even Job could not comfort Roniel. He stood at the corner of her chamber curtain, speaking softly, but she would not let him in.

"She will mend in time," I said to him, echoing Behira, and he turned back to his chambers, to ponder his fortunes and plan his next move.

"We will have to be careful not to let him burn too much oil at night," Behira whispered to me one day. "We are running low, and there is no money to buy new stores."

"It is an investment," I said. "We can afford some hope, at least, that our fortunes will change. God cannot mean to leave us so bereft."

Job stayed up late too often, he grew dim and irritable in the mornings, wheezing and then coughing— and then shaking with severe chills and fevers. At last he took to his bed, barely able to speak.

"What more can there be?" he said in a cracked voice as I bathed his forehead with a damp cloth and pulled his heavy blanket about his chin.

"It's the burden," I said, shushing him. "There has been much to bear, and even the mightiest falter under a heavy load."

He nodded at this, and slept fitfully. The next day the first of the boils appeared on his shoulder, red and purple. It gave him great pain, and he spent the day holding his arm gingerly.

"One blessing, the fever has passed," he said gruffly.

The boil was the first of many, and in the next few weeks they bloomed all over his body. Job grew more tired, and the fever returned. He took to his bed in long stretches. We called in expensive doctors whose cures did not work. Soon there was nothing left to support the servants and so we let them go, and Behira and I tended Job, making our trips to the market in shifts, to sell our wares and haggle for produce. Roniel kept to her chambers, and we left her alone except for the food we left outside her door.

"We cannot let her be forever," said Behira one day as we sat on opposite sides of Job's bed, watching his fitful slumber. "She does not eat even half of what we give her. She'll waste away."

"What can we do?" I asked, rubbing the bridge of my nose. For a while we had thought we could distract Roniel from her grief in little ways—inviting her to help with the housework, inventing reasons for her to go outside in the summer weather, even buying oranges at great price to tempt her from her seclusion. Nothing worked, and Roniel grew more pale each day.

"Perhaps things will improve soon, and we can take her away from this house," said Behira. "Things must improve soon—they cannot stay this horrible forever."

But as if to prove her wrong, things grew worse. Job's boils broke and ran with a foul-smelling pus that ruined his fine bedding and tainted the air in the house and yard with the stink of decay. He grew less alert as the pain increased, and more and more of the decisions of the household fell to Behira and myself. And still Roniel would not eat.

"We may have to force her to eat something," I said one evening as Behira and I rolled out our cushions in the common room—we had taken to sleeping there because the stench was not so great in the largest room. "I cannot bear the thought of doing it, but if we don't she may die."

"I don't blame her," said Behira in a cracked voice, lying down. "I am—not very hungry these days, either."

The next morning, the house was strangely quiet: we checked the rooms and found that Roniel was gone. For a brief, hopeful moment I thought perhaps she had at last broken through her storm of grief, but a look at Behira's face suggested a second, darker thought.

"I'm sure she is at the wells," I said, for it was mid-morning. "Or perhaps at Calev's—"

But Roniel was not at Calev's, nor at the wells, nor the market, nor the hills beyond Uz, nor any place that Behira and I searched in the days that followed. Job had slipped into the stupor of a fever again, and so one of us would stay with him while the other ranged the town and the surrounding lands, searching for Roniel or any who had word of her.

"It is perhaps too much to hope that she was taken like the prophet," said Behira quietly one night as we discussed where we might look next—and what we could tell Job when he awoke. His fever was wearing itself out at that time, and he had begun to call each of us by name.

"We will find her soon," I said, more for myself than Behira, though we both by now feared the worst.

It was Behira who found Roniel's headscarves at the river which fed the streams of Uz. They were rich fabric—it was unlikely she would have parted with them except as a final action, and had she been set upon by bandits, they would have taken the scarves with them.

"She must have thrown them as she leapt," I said, in sudden great exhaustion, sitting down as Behira brought the scarves to me, weeping.

"What will we tell Job?" she asked.

I bit my knuckle and for a second grief overtook me, and I wept with Behira. But I had learned the trick of sorrow, and soon my tears had dried and I said, "We must tell him, but say only that she has disappeared. That is all that we know, in any case."

We told Job that Roniel had disappeared, that we could not find her anywhere. But there is an understanding that grows up between men and women who have lived together for many years, and he took the meaning of our words. "Roniel, Roniel," he cried for many nights, and slipped back into his fever, where his dreams tormented him. In his waking hours we sought to comfort him, but there were few words of comfort that we could find.

One day when he was awake and I was bathing his boils, Job grabbed my hand and said, his eyes intense, "When will it end, Hadasa?" His grip was strong; it had only been stronger on that night the youths had come to tell us of our desolation.

I could only recite the saying of my grandmother: "Sorrow ends at death."

He nodded at that and was silent the rest of the day.

When word traveled through the town that Roniel was a suicide, the inhabitants of Uz began to treat us differently. People drew their coats about them more securely as we passed, and many did not return our greetings. Our coin was rapidly running out, and we were forced to buy more and more from the cheapest markets. But soon, even those merchants began to flinch as they saw Behira and me approach. Only Calev, the merchant whom Job had helped establish his business, kept his trade unhindered with us.

When I at last asked him why we were treated so, Calev sighed and said, "People fear that you have been cursed by God. It does not seem possible that your family should suffer so much disaster without there being cause."

"We have done no wrong," I said. "None that I know of. And if we have done ill, surely the many sacrifices we have sent should absolve us of any transgression we may have committed in ignorance." It was well-known in Uz that Job in his rich days did many sacrifices in fear of offending in ignorance.

Calev shrugged, uncomfortable. "I will continue to traffic with your household as long as I am able, Hadasa. But there are many that say that God will not be satisfied until he has reclaimed you all, and woe to anyone who helps you."

"God will not punish you for blessing our family with your friendship, Calev Bar-Jonas." I said, nettled.

He smiled. "I hope not. But still, the talk of the townspeople is powerful. If you could take Job somewhere away from here, where he was not so powerful and rich, then it may be best for you and your family."

"We have nowhere to go," I said, "not with Job as sick as he is."

Behira and I spoke of the incident later, as we made a thin soup from the onions I had purchased from

Calev. "We must bear being snubbed alongside the rest," said Behira.

"It is a small enough thing," I said in calm tones, though angry. "We can carry on unhindered as long as our family stays together."

But Calev was wiser than I recognized, and we were not left unhindered. It was not many nights later that there was a clap at our gate, loud and imperious. When I opened the door I saw a small mob of the citizens of Uz with our judge and his wife Elseba at their head.

"What is this honor?" I said, my heart sinking in my chest as I did so.

"Hadasa," said our judge, "may we see Job?"

"My husband is very ill," I said, my voice straining to carry over the crowd. "And even if he were not, he could not see so many. What is your business?"

There were murmurs from the crowd. The judge—he was an officious man—said, "We must speak to him," as he turned the rings on his fingers.

"He is ill," I repeated. "I can give him your message, if you like."

Someone from the crowd called what the judge would not. "Job must leave Uz! We cannot have him stay here!"

I cast my eyes about for the speaker, but he was lost in the crowd. "Why should we leave our house and the lands we've lived in all our lives?"

The judge spoke at last. "The disease may spread, Hadasa. There are our children and our crops to think of. We have to ask you to move him."

"If the disease would spread, wouldn't his wives come down with it as well?" I asked. "We will not move because there is illness in the world. You should be ashamed for asking." For a second I stared down the crowd, and then stepped back into the house and shut the door.

"God is punishing him," said a woman's voice from outside—I think it was Elseba's. "We do not want to be punished alongside him."

"God is wise enough to keep the cup of punishment from spilling over," I said through the door. "It is enough that God has turned against this house—will our neighbors turn against us also?"

"He must leave," said the man again. "We cannot have a curse at the center of the town."

I would have held the door against them for as long as my frail body would have stood the battering, but at that moment Behira came to me and said in her soft voice that Job wished to leave.

"He says that if his kinsmen all agree, he must bend to their will," she said.

I sagged against the door, still listening to the rabble outside. "Where would he have us go?"

Behira bit her lip. "There is the potter's shed we own, beyond the town. It isn't much, but it's somewhere to go to and it's near to the wells. We can go there until we think of what to do next."

"It isn't right," I hissed, but Behira could not answer that, so together we went to Job and between ourselves carried him to the doorway. The crowd drew away from us but did not flee. Even in the open night air the stench from Job's sores was incredible.

"You see how little power he has to harm you?" I shouted to the crowd. It was not my place, and Job whispered, "Hadasa, Hadasa."

The crowd did not answer me. We stepped, excruciatingly slow, from our fine house and down the main road of Uz. Job drooped with each step, and the juice of his sores ran on our arms. Someone from the crowd threw a stone, there were broken murmurs. It was badly thrown, if it were meant for Job; it struck Behira in the face, drawing a dark well of blood in a line across her cheek.

If it had been myself and not Behira, I could have borne it. But the fire of wrong was already in me, and so I left Job sagging in Behira's arms and flew at the crowd, nearly sobbing, nearly screaming, "Is there any here who has been wronged by my husband or my house? Stand and make witness, if you have anything to say. If anyone dares to make a case against us to the elders, I will bear the punishment for my family to the last pebble." There was no reply, though some of the crowd drew away into the shadows under the houses.

"Hadasa," said Job again, and I returned to help him up and together Behira and I carried him through the streets of Uz toward the distant potter's shed. The crowd behind us dispersed the further we stepped, but none came forward to aid us, and there was still a small clot of people as we stepped out beyond the boundaries of Uz. It was not until we laid Job in the dirty corner of the potter's shed and I stepped to its doorway that I saw that the citizens of Uz had disappeared, as if they had never been.

I returned three times to our house that night, under cover of darkness, to gather some meager bedding and clothes and food to support us, as well as bandages for Job and for Behira's face. It was well I did, for the next day the citizens of Uz burned our household goods, in fear of disease.

I had managed only the barest of supplies. "We will have to find something to eat," I said as we huddled on the floor of the hut.

Behira was quiet, her face swaddled in dark bandages.

"Perhaps Calev would help us," I said, standing and pacing, for I could not sit for long without feeling as if I would snarl with the unfairness and indignity of our situation. "I will ask him for some few things once our stores have run out."

I approached Calev in the market the next week.

"Are you well, Hadasa?" he asked.

"We are alive, Calev," I responded. "But we need food. I cannot work for it and our stores have been consumed by our sorrows. You said once you would help us as long as you were able."

Calev sighed. "I can't support two families on what I make, Hadasa. Should my child turn sick, or the market run low—"

"I know how thin the curtain is that keeps us from ruin, Calev," I said.

He tapped his nose, not smiling. "Pretty words won't pay for cabbages."

"Words are the only thing we have left." I lowered my eyes. "I'm not asking you. I'm begging."

He sighed. "I would like to help you, Hadasa—"

I grabbed his arm, he did not flinch away. "Then you can help us, Calev. Job showed us that—if nothing else, Job showed us that. I know he has given to you. It is your blessing to give in return."

He hesitated, then nodded. "Very well," he said—and we had food for another day.

Through this time, Behira hardly spoke at all. It was as if the stone had silenced her—Behira, who sang once of nightingales and wildflowers. She spent her days wrapping and unwinding Job in his gray bandages, cleaning his seeping sores with what fabric we could salvage from Uz's pits. When she was not with him she was cleaning his soiled blankets and bandages; scrubbing them between stones when the citizens of Uz turned us away from the stream for fear the disease would spread.

I do not know which one of us had the more difficult time in those days—me with my face to the world, cringing and gleaning and picking through the refuse for our starved existence, or Behira, who sat unflinching in the stench and the cloud of Job's mute sorrow. Job wept helplessly when his bandages were changed, and spoke of death when he rested, but did little else. It was up to Behira and me to be all and do all to make sure that our tiny family could still struggle on, morning after morning.

"Behira," I asked one day when we sat for a rare moment of rest in the doorway of the hut, our aching backs against the frame, "would you like to go to town—would you like—a day away from him?" I feared for a moment she would accuse me of disloyalty, but she looked at me with her kind eyes and I saw that she understood.

"No," she said, shaking her head. Her voice was husky from disuse. "It keeps me from running away, sitting with him, it keeps me from disappearing . . . like Roniel . . . "

"How?" I thought how old my voice sounded, how small and cracked.

She smiled, a soft, sad smile. "I tie a bandage for my children—one for Margalit, and Alon, and Harel, and little Kochaua. I tie one for you, and for your children, and for Roniel and her son Gidon. I tie one for—for him." Job was so silent and changed that we had begun to speak of him like a natural thing, the way a farmer might speak of the sun or the rain, something beyond comprehension or appeal. We rarely spoke his name. "Sometimes," Behira continued, a quiet blush creeping onto her pale, starved face, "there's a bandage left over, and I tie that one for a child that may be, for the future . . . "

Her voice was beautiful again, and I turned away. My grief was pawing at my heart, and I could not afford to give way.

"Hadasa, how do you remember your children?" Behira's voice was far away.

"I can't allow myself to remember them," I said, and I sounded so old

it was amazing to me that I did not turn to dust and blow away in the desert breeze. "There is so much to do, and we must be strong."

"Dear Hadasa," she said, and her hand found mine even though her eyes bore unblinking into the hills far away.

And then it was harvest time, and I was gone from the hut more and more often, for it is a custom in the land of Uz to leave the corners of the fields for the destitute, and as God had only cursed my family there was plenty of food to be had for the rich and the poor. I thanked God again and again that we had observed the gleanings when we stood at the forefront of Uz, for now it looked like we would survive the winter with the ears we could pick from what was left of the main harvest. Behira would smile, even, when I came with bushels of grain to be packed carefully in the corners of the hut—a quiet, suffocated smile, but a true smile. Job, lost in his pain, recognized what he could of the blessing we had been given. With the work and the food, I began to feel that if we were not being blessed by God, he was at least letting us go our way and survive as best we could.

Job chided me for this, when I spoke to him as Behira and I washed him with the water we carried from the wells one day. Bathing gave him momentary respite from his pain, and we kept him as clean as we could, soaking his bandages in water and wiping him carefully, making use of each precious drop.

"It is God's blessing, this water," he said as we swabbed his chest.

"It is your wives' blessing," I said, to tease him. "God provides the sores, and the wives to clean the sores away."

"You should not speak lightly," said Job, again thunderous with right, as he had been in the old days before his sorrows.

I thrilled to see him awaken, so I said, "God perhaps has left our family, but we have not left each other. We will make it through."

"That's foolish, Hadasa," he said sternly. "Should we assume that God has abandoned us, because we are not rich or healthy? It may be that God has his purposes in this illness, which I cannot yet see."

"Meanwhile, your wives can see your back needs washing, so turn over—if you can," I said, and together we helped him roll over to his front, him crying out weakly the whole way. We set to work on his back, our hands working the bandages in careful unison.

Job surprised us by speaking. "God is testing me," he said quietly.

We paused. Behira looked to me, I took an uncertain breath. "He cannot be testing you, Job. Is there any man more loyal to God than you are?"

"Perhaps that is what he is testing."

"That seems very—cruel—to me," I said, returning to my bathing and motioning Behira to do the same.

"God is not like man, he does not think as man does," said Job, gasping as we attacked his sores.

"Perhaps not," I said. "Be still."

"Perhaps God will keep me alive as long as I do not curse him or speak ill of him."

Behira was crying, quietly. I said, "Perhaps God must make his own decisions, Job," more curtly than I meant to.

"What do you think, Hadasa?"

This was a new thing for Job, to ask for my opinion, and I surprised myself by saying what I thought. "It seems to me that God should know what a man suffers, and not leave a good man in pain." And then my sorrow sank into me and I had to be up and out of the hut, to lean against the wall and cry my bit in great gasping sobs.

It was later that Behira came to me where I sat against the wall. She sat next to me and leaned against my shoulder. "He is sorry," she said quietly.

"We are all sorry," I croaked, "but none of us is to blame." We sat there for a long time, watching the stars in their sharp clusters.

It grew colder, and Behira and I slept huddled together for warmth, giving our few bare blankets to Job. The cold turned my bones against each other—they ached and seemed to grind at their joints. The fields gave out, and went fallow, and I turned back to begging. It was more difficult—Calev was having his own difficulties and could give less, and the other land-owners in town repeated their claims that Job was being punished by God and that they didn't dare help a man whom God had turned against. I wept, I groveled, I called on them to witness the good that Job had done for Uz, but they were stone. I turned to waiting for the scraps of the market and hunting the scrub for food. There was little enough, and as it got colder, there was less.

One night, I woke up to Behira's screams. She was half-asleep, and sobbing, great horrible cries that wracked her entire body and left her shivering.

"What, what is it?" cried Job thinly from his spot on the floor.

"It's Behira," I said, shaking her. She clung to me and kept at her sobbing, awake now, wild-eyed, her graying hair in tatters about her face.

"What is wrong?" asked Job, struggling to rise.

"I don't know, Job," I said.

Behira was lost to me, though I called to her she sobbed and shook and could not hear.

"Behira, Behira," said Job, and that she heard, and it set her to sobbing louder.

"I will take her outside," I said as firmly as I dared. "She needs some air. Will you—will you be all right?"

"Behira," he said, tears coursing down his ruined face, then nodded. "I will be all right."

I gathered up Behira—how thin she had become, who used to have so much life inside of her, and together we stumbled out of the potter's hut and to the desert beyond, where the air was clean and sharp. We wandered over the rough land, nearly losing our footing on the hard earth, until we came to a gentle hill where I sat us down so we could be quiet and alone.

Behira wept till the thin moon was beyond the hills, and I comforted her as best I could, standing as much as I could like a wall between her and Uz, the hut, and the world. And all the time she wept I thought of the Behira who had been, and her bright eyes and beautiful voice, and I felt that it was not possible that God could not know who Behira was.

So when at last she was done, and she sat in the quiet exhaustion that comes from tears, I said with a heavy voice, "Behira, you must go home to your people. You still have family in Beth-channan."

She shook her head heavily. "I couldn't, Hadasa."

"You must." I took her by the shoulders. "Job is dying, Behira. He cannot last through the winter. It is no shame to return home a widow. Job will die, and I may die too—there is nothing much more that I care for, than to finish this last duty. But I can't bear to see my whole family get ground to pieces under this millstone. You have youth, you have beauty, still—you can live again in Beth-channan and think of us." I took a breath, strangely clear as the night sky. "You must go. I think I will die if you don't live again."

She was too spent to cry at that, but she said in a tiny voice, "How can I go, and spend my whole life missing Job and you?" and I wept at that, and she held me this time and was my wall against the world.

We went back to the hut and the next day we carried on as we had always done. But she knew that she must go—she knew as soon as I had said it, I think. Soon we heard of a merchant travelling to Beth-channan, and Behira left with one of my scarves in her hands as a memory and with Job's blessing. I helped him to the doorway of the hut when she left, and he waved to her feebly as she walked away on unsteady legs.

"Will everyone go away?" he asked in his quaking voice.

"I will not," I said, and helped him back inside.

With the end of the harvest season, the friends Job had made in the towns surrounding Uz found the time to come and comfort him in his sickened state. He received messages from them saying such things as "Bildad is coming" in their crabbed scripts, and it set him to worrying, which inflamed his skin and broke him into rashes under his sores.

"It would be better to be dead than to be sick, weak—like a baby—in front of my friends," he said one morning as I changed his bandages.

I was tired, and not paying much heed to what he said. With Behira gone, I had twice the duties as before, and I slept little. "It may be better to be dead," I said, unwinding a loop of fabric, "but if one is alive it is better to have friends."

"We shall have to serve them food," he said.

I stopped winding. "There is no food to serve them, Job."

He winced. "Nevertheless, it is our duty. To not serve them would be an insult to God, their creator."

"What insult?" I put down the bandages. "What do the starving owe the fed? Job, why maintain your integrity? You are no longer a rich man—they do not expect you to feast them."

"Nevertheless," he said again,

sighing.

"Never our less," I said, standing. "Job, they are coming to comfort you. I cannot find food for so many."

He sighed. "Why are we so troubled, Hadasa? I can remember a time when it was a joy to give to our friends, now it is a hardship. Still"—and I think he said this more to himself than to me—"we are judged for our times of hardship, not our times of ease."

"True words, husband," I said, my heart breaking, "but they won't create food from broken pots."

He was silent. His illness sometimes took him suddenly—I looked and saw that he was weeping. I went to him and held his head in my lap, filthy and oozing though it was.

"I want to die, Hadasa," he whispered. "God won't let me die."

"I know, I know," I shushed him, stroking his gray hair. "God is mindful of you, even still."

"What does He have in his mind, though?" he asked. His eyes were always very blue—in his fever, they burned as if the very sky were in flames. "What does He want from me?"

"Perhaps he doesn't want anything from you," I said. "Men can be sick without God asking them for something, we know that."

"He won't let me die," he repeated. "He won't let me die

unless I break and curse him." He twisted in my hands in a small scream.

I thought I would be overcome, in my exhaustion and hunger and my love for my husband, who wracked himself against the floor. "Oh, Job, Job," I said, and I do not blush to repeat it—"If that is what he is waiting for, can you not curse him and find your peace? Surely, God would not punish you forever for one deed, after a life of nothing but good?"

"Is it punishment?" he said, weeping. "I don't know. I do not know."

I wiped my eyes. "You will feel better when there is food, and when you may meet with your friends. I will go find meat, it's the season for it, and all will be well."

He nodded, his blue eyes full.

I wept my own helpless tears on my way to the market, but by that time helpless tears were daily fare, and they did not slow my step. The market was closed—it was too late in the year for begging. Drawing my breath up the way a rich woman might gather her robes around her, I went to the home of Elseba.

Her lady-servant showed me to her chamber—there were drapes on the walls against the winter chill and small caskets of her jewelry. For a second my breath left me—I had forgotten what wealth looked like.

Elseba sat with her back to me,

arranging her hair in a copper mirror. She did not turn to greet me, but said as I came in, "Hadasa, I am so glad you've come. Please, come in, be comfortable."

"I am happy to speak with the porters," I said, my eyes on the ground.

"We are friends, Hadasa," said Elseba, her voice mellow. "Why should we communicate through servants?" She finished at her table and turned around to face me. "Now, then—what do you wish?"

I set my teeth. "Whatever you can spare would be a blessing, Elseba."

She laughed, a warm sound. "We can spare a great many things. Do you need clothes to meet your friends in? Cushions for them to sit on?"

"Food is all we need. Thank you."

She laughed again. "Are you sure? I'm certain that I could find trappings for your home that could make your guests more comfortable. They are all quite rich, are they not?"

"You are very kind," I said. "Food is all we require, though. We do not need more than that."

"Very well, then—" Elseba waved her hand eloquently. "It has been so long since I put a simple meal together. Tell me—what will you require?"

"If we could have a bit of meat, that should do well, Elseba."

Elseba considered me. "Food is very dear right now."

"If it is too great a thing to ask, I will ask elsewhere," I said. "I am grateful for your consideration of me and my family." Already my mind looked ahead to whom I could ask next, though if meat were dear it may be a struggle till the end.

"Oh, Hadasa," laughed Elseba. "You simply surprised me. I felt sure you would ask for something less . . . celebratory. But we have had some fortune this year, and I am sure something can be done for you." She regarded me again, a slow sweep of her narrowed eyes. "I believe we may have a leftover shank of goat from our feast yesterday. Will that do for you and your friends?"

I could not help but smile in gratitude, and for the first time I looked at Elseba in her face. "Yes, Elseba, that would do very well."

"Well, then," she said, and with a negligent wave of her hands turned back to her vanity. "Have the porters wrap it for you, and best of blessings to you and your friends."

A whole goat shank! It is impossible to describe the preciousness of its weight in my arms. There would be enough for days; we could eat meat for nearly a week if we were careful. The deed was done, I had debased myself and been rewarded, and though my tears still flowed on the way to the potter's shed, they were tears of relief. Job's integrity had been saved, and Elseba's delighted pity was now only a memory.

The scribes have written much about the visit of Job's friends but I have little to say of it; as it is unseemly for a woman of Uz to keep conversation with men, I stood in our small yard and cooked, and did my work mending my clothes and tearing whatever couldn't be mended into long bandages for Job. His friends came late in the day and stayed late into the night, but mercifully they did not eat much; more mercifully they did not bring gifts of charity, which would have shamed Job beyond endurance. I remember most of the days as being dull—the soft rumble of voices from within the hut, now raised, now reasonable, and the slow slide of the sun from one horizon to the next. One day there was a sudden rain—it was winter, after all. I sat under the eaves of the roof and watched the sandy earth bounce in the falling water. There was the bread to make on the board, under the white clouds, and the fire to keep going in the kiln. The most active part of the day was the comings and goings, our kindly old friends made alien in the squalor of our poverty. Here was Zophar, sweeping as ever, his merry voice booming in our hut; Bildad

with his formal speech (he has royalty in his family) unconsciously smoothing his silks in the dust; Eliphaz with his quick, self-conscious smile; Elihu looking still like a blushing boy, though he was nearing his fourth decade. They were kind enough to greet Job with smiles and warm jokes—the spectacle of their arrival would have been too much without it. Job was grateful, I think, to speak with men again, and we both gave thanks that his fever had broken for a few days, that he could sit and listen and speak to them of great truths as he had done before our troubles.

Only one task I had to perform— to make the food, and that was peace and rest. That, and to beg them each in turn not to draw back from the smell of Job's illness. He had long ago grown used to it, and he could not have borne the shame of their horror. They let their eyes water and I thanked God for them.

On the third day of their visit, Bildad, our oldest family friend, pulled me aside as I swept the ground about the hut.

"He is very low," he said.

I laughed, for I could not help it, at his dark expression. "Oh, Bildad— he is very well today. He sits up, he speaks. It is a great blessing."

He nodded, biting his lip. "Has there been—what I mean to say—"

He was very earnest. I pulled my shawl about me and looked at him as levelly as I dared.

"Hadasa, you are his wife and have seen his woes from the beginning," he said at last, sighing. "Do you know of any sin he may have committed—even unwittingly—that could have caused God to have punished him so greatly?"

"If there was sin, we have both committed it, Bildad," I said as gently as I could. "If there is sin in following God as best as can be managed by imperfect creatures, then we have sinned. We are not perfect—but we do not sin if we can help it."

He nodded, but I could see that it worried him, and I wondered what Job and his friends said.

On the seventh day, I could tell by the rumble of voices that their arguments were coming to their end, but still there was some heat in their tones and the speeches began to drag out in the manner of men who know they have made their point but are not willing to let go of the beauty of their argument. Evening gathered as they spoke, and then night, and the bone-turning cold of the desert settled in.

It was not long before it grew too cold to sit and wait, and I began to pace around our tiny hut, rubbing my arms against the chill. The moonlight was blue on the cold desert earth, and the bare yellow stalks of the summer plants sent black shadows stabbing across the ground. The moon was sailing over Uz, and even at this hour, a few torches were glimmering among the houses. It could have even been a feast day for what I remembered of the passage of time.

At once the city and the hut oppressed me, almost so that I couldn't breathe, and I turned and walked out into the desert over the hardscrabble hills. I had some vague thought that I would go and sit where Behira and I had sat, many months before—but when I came to the spot I passed it by without hesitation. In time I climbed over the furthest hills, and soon Uz winked out of existence into the shadows behind me. I knew that at any moment Job's friends could leave and he would look for me, but for the moment it was peace to stretch my legs, to get away from the city in which I had suffered so much.

There were dangers in the open desert—bold jackals, stinging insects, and bands of marauders. But our troubles had been stalking me all day, and fear of being captured by them kept me stumbling over the grainy earth.

But I could not run forever, and at last I collapsed in the crook of an overhanging bluff, and there my sorrow at last overtook me and consumed me. I wept, then, loudly and wild-eyed like a mourner does, though my grief was now old and the world in which I had been a mother of children seemed almost like another's life. But as I thought of each of my children they grew warmer and more alive to me, and at the last I wept and screamed as if they had perished moments before. And then at last there were no more tears and no more voice for screams, and I sat huddled in the crook of the embankment, an old woman with a hoarse voice staring blankly at the stars.

It grew later, but my thoughts did not grow weary; indeed, they did not seem to move at all. My grief sat as implacable as a stone in my throat, and soon all there was to my thought was the sound of my own breath, the blank world around me, and my bones setting themselves against each other in the cold.

It was not until much later that I noticed the sky was streaming with light, as if hundreds of stars had suddenly leapt from their place and were dancing toward Uz. It was so unexpected and so beautiful that I felt in some startled way that my grief had shaken the very stars from the sky. The stars were speeding away from me and toward Uz, traversing the two leagues I had traveled to speed toward Job and his friends huddled in our tiny hut, toward Calev and his unruly children, toward Elseba slumbering on

her fine linens.

Even the stars flee from pain, I thought in near-stupor, recalling then what Job said before our troubles began, that success attracted more and more success, that good actions brought good actions. Tears once again pricked my eyes, stinging and warm.

I cannot hope to explain on my own the thing which happened next to me. But it seemed suddenly as if along with the stars something great and joyous and tragic were walking on the earth toward Uz, as if the desert itself were rising up to surge toward my home with all its hidden warmth and sharp sands. The land suddenly rolled in unexpected scents—the round freshness of spring, the tang of rotting flesh. All these things were around me for a moment, and then the Presence passed by, on toward Uz. I felt it go as I might watch a caravan pass—the certainty of it was a greater certainty than sight affords.

I wanted to cry to the Presence to return, to stay with me, to come and give me comfort. But my voice was too small for the enormity of that unseen creature, and so I sat with my mouth open. And in the absence of the Presence, it seemed suddenly as if I were under a great scrutiny, as if I were naked in the desert and every part of me was exposed to light indifferently. My being was measured and separated, the way a woman might separate the organs of a goat upon the cleaning board. I saw at once as I was seen by the eye of the world, all of me at once—my jealousy of Elseba, my uncertain courage, my love for Job bound up in flashes of resentment and bitterness. I felt a great Seeing pass over me again and again and felt its great indifference for me, how unremarkable I seemed to it, how uninteresting. Seeing myself as it saw me, I felt the same: Here is an old woman, no better or no worse than most, I thought, though she is very sad.

And then the whole earth—the desert, its plants, the dark sky, the swollen moon—spoke to me with a single voice.

"You have been asking questions," said the voice of the desert. "Hadasa, you have asked many things."

"I have tried not to," I said, my voice tiny in that greatness. "I have tried to believe as Job does."

The voice was cool as a smooth stone in shadow. "Job is a faithful servant."

"He thinks that if he doesn't resent being hurt, doesn't recoil from being stung, that God will spare him," I said with more heat than I had intended. "I am the weaker of the two of us, I am hurt too easily. I am too easily overcome by grief."

"What do you know of grief?" it

asked.

This seemed too large a question to answer. "My family was taken," I weakly responded.

The voice had no pitch or timbre. "Whole nations fall under heaven; what is your family to them?"

"I only know what I have felt, Lord."

"What have you felt?" asked the voice. "A woman's feelings—nothing more. A mother fox would feel the same were her pups drowned in a spring flood. You won't shake heaven with grief—Roniel has already tried. Hadasa, where is Roniel? Where has she gone?"

"She felt too much," I said, miserable. "She has disappeared."

"Roniel cursed God." The voice was a whisper that thundered.

I began to weep again, foolishly, for Roniel. "She was young and afraid—and out of herself with grief."

"Dry your tears," said the voice, unmoved. "What can this wetness mean to the world?"

"We disappear when we have no place to live, Lord. We cannot live in a world where greater disaster than we can bear follows every thing we may have done to be upright. It isn't fair to punish her for her sorrow and desperation."

"What is fair?" asked the voice. "Does the ripening wheat find the harvest fair? Does the kid think it fair that the wolf hunts her? Will you set the whole world on its side so that it is fair to the wife of an inconsequential merchant of Uz?"

"What are we to do, then, Lord?" I asked.

"You have the law," said the voice. "You know your place within it. What knowledge do you have that is greater than the word of God?"

"None," I said, my hands clenching. "I do not seek to commit blasphemy."

"And yet you have done so, just the same," said the voice. "You set yourself up to lecture the heavens on what is fair. But what have you done, Hadasa, to deserve the position you have claimed as your own? You cannot even turn aside Job's illness, or save your family from lightning, and these are very small matters in the wide world."

"They are not small to me."

"The pebble is not small to the ant," said the voice. "Shall the law be rewritten for every creature that stumbles across an obstacle?"

"But what benefit is there, Lord," I asked, "if those who follow the law are not protected from harm and sorrow?"

"What do you know of law?" The voice surged through the desert. "Do you know the law that causes one crop to grow and another to wither? Do you claim that because the stream flows downhill it is unfair to the uplands? Do you know the laws of life and death because you have seen a child born or a goat slaughtered? Speak wisely, or not at all—the law of God is greater than the narrow strip of land you tread on."

As the voice spoke I had come to a conclusion: At its speaking to me I felt a fierce despair that I had never felt before or since. The voice died away and I drew myself up and said to the desert: "Very well." My voice was startling in its strength and clarity, but I did not flinch. I was not angry, as you might suppose, but something had solidified inside me, something heavy and hard, and with it inside me I did not fear the voice.

"What is 'very well', Hadasa?" it asked.

"I see that there is no hope to be who I am and to not curse God, if it is cursing God to feel hurt when his fire destroys my life. If I cannot hope for God's approval then I must do what I can on my own."

"And what will you do?" asked the voice.

"I will tend to Job until his death," I said. "It cannot be very far away now."

"And then?"

"And then—I will follow Roniel to the grave. What else?"

For answer there was nothing but wind, perhaps a whispered laugh, and at once I was alone in the desert.

The night was still cold but I felt on fire with energy, my bones for once solid in my frame. I began to walk home in great strides, my headscarves flying in the wind. I think I could have wrestled a wolf had I encountered one—there was such strength in me that almost I thought I could live the law the voice had reminded me of, now that I knew it was pointless. It was as if a great door had shut inside me, quietly and irrevocably sealing me off from fear and pain. God could batter me about as he would now, I thought, and the worst I could do would be to die. I could take suffering without complaint, be mute in the face of hurt. Indeed, in my cold passion I felt no need to ever speak again.

I do not think that I would have kept my resolve long—life does not let us cling to clarity. But I may have made a decision that night that changed my life forever, had I not stepped sideways on an unstable stone and been thrown forward onto the hard earth below.

The shock of the pain of it (I scraped my arm badly on the stones I stumbled over) was so great that for an instant my iron will disappeared and I laughed a great dry laugh. And though I picked myself up again and resumed my resolute walk across the desert, the fervor I had felt before had been tempered, and I no longer felt the need to race towards my fate.

Resolution is poor company. The more I walked toward Uz the less interested I became in my new-found certainty, and the more lonely I became. And so, in a bored way, I envisioned how a friend and I would talk about my resolve, if it had happened long ago before my troubles.

"I'll not ever break," I said to her, half fiercely. "I'll be strong till the end."

The response was a laugh, as warm and beautiful as Behira's laugh, though Behira would never have laughed at me being angry with God. "Oh, Hadasa," said my imaginary friend, "you have done so many miraculous things in the past year. But you cannot stay angry with God forever. It isn't in your nature."

I said, "It isn't anger—I must be strong to save my life. I can keep from feeling if I choose."

"That is so," admitted my friend. "Will you choose to?"

"How can I choose anything else?" I asked. "God doesn't punish us through fire or poverty or disease—it is through the things we feel that he torments us. If God chooses to be my enemy, how can I do anything else but build a fortress in my heart against him?"

"Job would say something else."

"I am not Job," I said. "And I wish the world would not compare us. He thinks of his illness as a problem he can solve, with death or prayer or discussion with his friends. He thinks that if he can answer the riddle of God's behavior, then God will reward him."

"What do you think, Hadasa?"

The voice in my head was suddenly so like Job's that I stopped and stared about the empty, moonlit desert. The yellowed weeds tossed in a slight breeze in the split rocks; the heavy moon sat brooding over distant Uz.

"I think," I said to the desert, "that it is a very wicked God who hands his children puzzles that wreck their hearts and take the lives of their families. It is an unreasonable God who demands we never ask him why we are arbitrarily blessed and punished. And it is a selfish God who insists that we love him as he hurts us again and again. And there at last I have spoken clear blasphemy, and God will now destroy me for it."

I sat down on a nearby rock and sighed, crossing my feet. My throat felt scrubbed and raw, and in the absence of feeling there was a strange peace. I was content to rest in the quiet of the desert.

The voice in my head had not vanished. "Waiting for the end?" it asked, the hint of a smile in its tone.

I laughed, and for the first time in many days to laugh felt warm and alive, not forced through the constriction of my troubles. "Is there anything else to be done? Job and I have nothing beyond the end to hope for."

"He needs you a great deal."

"Does he?" I smiled, thinking of Job's mild surety, his warm convictions, his surprising moments of self-doubt. "Yes, I suppose he does."

"And not just in his illness. He needed you long before that— perhaps from the beginning. He loved you and respected you always."

It appeared that even in my head, no one could describe me without Job. I sighed and said, "Job is a good man."

My friend caught my sigh. "You resent him?"

I shrugged. "At times. He presses away pain with his piety, asks me to bear both his pain and his righteousness. Is it wrong to be resentful of his goodness?"

"Is it?" The voice was warm. "Could you help feeling resentful from time to time?"

"I could try."

"Yes, you could. But it is not a strange thing for people who live together to resent each other from time to time. Does it change much, your resentment? Are you more sharp with him, less forgiving? Do you love him less?"

"No. I love him the same."

"Well, then," my friend said.

I sighed again. "It felt at one point that God was part of the love we had together, and now it feels as if my love for Job is my only defense against the troubles which God has sent upon us. Why has God abandoned us?"

My friend was surprised. "Has he?"

"It feels so." I rubbed my elbow, where the bones ached. "Is it strange that I can say these things to you and have it not feel like blasphemy? We have suffered so much—for us, I mean, not in relation to others. We have done our best, but it feels as if we have no comfort."

"You have been very strong."

"Strong!" I snorted. "It doesn't feel strong."

"How does it feel, Hadasa?"

"Oh—desperate, and sad. As if I were caught about to give birth, and had no midwife present."

"In what way?"

"In that there is this grief within me that struggles to break free, but there is none to help me bear it."

"You do not wish for your wealth to return, then?"

I laughed, again a warm sound. "Of course I do. But we have done as well as paupers as we did wealthy—we have not starved, and we have not turned on each other. That is what is important, perhaps."

"You miss your children."

"How could I not? Who can understand what it is like to lose her whole family in one horrible moment?"

"God, perhaps," said my friend. "The flood was a terrible moment."

"I can't compare myself to God," I said. "I always suffer by the comparison. And so I must carry my grief alone, without hope of deliverance."

My friend was silent. I could see that the sky was lightening, so I stood slowly and once again began to walk the way toward Uz, hobbling a little.

"Hadasa," said my friend from behind me.

And so I turned and saw that the friend I had been speaking to was the Presence, that it had returned to give me comfort after all. The Presence stood in front of me in the growing light, its arms open, beseeching.

"Oh—" I said, and in that word there was more of my mourning than all of my hours of weeping. I was dumbstruck, not by the Presence but by the unexpectedness of it returning to me, of coming to me after the darkness of the desert night. Pain rushed out of me, leaving me light and breathless.

"Hadasa," said the Presence, "Hadasa, you have been very sorrowful. I am sorry for your pain, so very sorry."

I wanted to be abashed. Certainly, I was humbled by standing before such greatness and majesty. But I had spoken so long and so warmly with the Presence that I could not fall to my knees. So I stared, my mouth open.

"Will you forgive me?" asked the Presence.

"You ask me for forgiveness?" I said at last. "What have I done to deserve your apology?"

"What have you done to deserve your troubles, Hadasa? The world is not built on a ledger. Once I was loved by you and now I am not. I wish to be forgiven."

"But you—" I laughed, shortly, as a woman who knocks her shin against a tent pole. "I cannot forgive you, for you cannot do anything wrong."

"That is the main thing, perhaps, that I wish to be forgiven of."

I sat again. "How should I forgive you? Do you wish for me to say it is all right that you took my children and struck my husband down with a wasting disease?"

"I have asked for forgiveness, Hadasa, not for you to tell me what things are right. I am not admitting wrong."

"Isn't that what an apology is?" I asked.

"Is it?" said the Presence. "Is Job's faith wrong? And yet you must forgive him of it as much as you must forgive Elseba her near-sightedness."

I looked at my hands. "It is hard, Lord, to lose my children. It seems a greater punishment than I deserve."

The Presence's voice grew warmer, lighter. "You have suffered much—misery and doubt. But I cannot tell you if what you have borne is more or less than your share, for there are no guidelines set for that. There is no punishment, Hadasa, in what you suffer. The laws that govern the world are larger than spite."

"You should have spared my children." I was surprised by the anger with which I said this, the ugliness of my tone. "What good is the law when my children have been taken from me?"

"What is the good of a law which is partial to one woman's children over another's? Not every thing that happens on this earth is a symptom of favor or punishment. Death and life come to everyone in turn—young and old, rich and poor. Everyone pleads, when hardship comes, that it be turned away from those that they love. For whom should we make an exception?"

"They were so young—they had their whole lives ahead of them."

The Presence's voice was gentle. "You know, then, how long their lives were meant to be?"

"But why me?" I asked in a sudden cold fury, my hands in fists in my lap. "Why have you singled me out to bear blow after blow, to stand in public shame in the market, to tend my husband as he suffers, to be childless and without a future? What can you possibly hope to prove through this torment, except the precise moment when we weak creatures will break under you? Are you the greater for our misery, more masterful because we cannot turn against you? Have you spared Job and me and Behira and Roniel and our children no thought? Have you no compassion? Have you no feeling?" My head burned with fury, and I said, "Sometimes, I think I hate you!"

I spoke these terrible things in a hiss, barely daring to look at the Presence, but at the same time unable to take my eyes away. And when I had finished speaking there was a silence far more frightening than my words had been, and almost I thought I would be blasted away in anger, like the sand before a storm.

But I was not destroyed, for to my surprise the Presence was weeping, weeping like a mother who has lost her child.

In my home lands of Shuhua we have a story that mothers tell to keep their children from striking each other in anger. In it, a man plants a field of barley to make his fortune. The first year, the sun scorches the plants and the crop fails. The man says, "My son's laziness has made the crop fail," and beats him. The second year, the rains come and drown the crops, and the man says, "My son's incompetence has made the crop fail," and beats him again. At last, in the third year the barley grows straight and true, but at the last moment a pestilence touches the man's crops and they are ruined before the harvest. And so the man beats his son until his son is nearly dead. And when the man realizes his only son is nearly dead, he cries in anguish, "Oh, son—why did you let me beat you to death? Why did you not fight back?" To which the son replies, "Because, father, you must beat something, and you could not beat the sun or the rains or the pestilence."

Standing before the Presence, this story occurred to me suddenly and with force, the way that stories from our childhood often do. I saw at once what my protestations of grief amounted to, and how little my tears had been for my children or for Job, and I staggered with the weight of it.

"I have been selfish, Lord," I said at last.

The Presence still wept, but said, "Not all selfishness is evil. It is not wrong to have your self wrapped up in your love, not wicked to feel attacked when the whirlwind howls."

"I wish, though—" I bit my lip.

"What do you wish, Hadasa?"

"I do not want my memory of my children and my husband to be bound up in frustration and rage and pique. I wish to grieve for them honestly, and completely."

"That is a noble desire."

"Will you—will you teach me how?"

And then it seemed as if the world around the Presence swelled into one great crescendo, and the Presence said, "Oh, Hadasa—" and pulled me into its arms, and I knew at once that God knew my name, and the names of my children, and that he kept his eye on Behira and Job and even Roniel. And then I knew and knew, and it seemed there could be no end to the things that I saw for the first time.

I cannot write much of what transpired from the moment the Presence took me into its arms. These written words are not sufficient; there is little enough that can be shared with them . . . it is a thing the scribes do not yet know, that God cannot be found in what has been written. Words are only the sign toward the path, a knocker on the door frame. I do not see, now, how we confuse them so.

I cannot say when the Presence disappeared exactly, for it was not like that—for though my knowledge of it dimmed as the world lightened, I did not feel the pain of a departure. There was a time when I felt the Presence less keenly, that was all, and in that sense I woke again to the world as it had been in the night before.

It was a beautiful dawn, and for all my discomfort from a sleepless night I felt refreshed. Already the sun warmed the hardscrabble earth, and as I stretched it felt as if my aching bones resumed their places and were reprieved. But with my new strength came again the realization of how dangerous the desert was, and how far away I was from my home and kinsmen. And so, though I longed to wander the brightening hills, I turned toward the city of Uz and walked as speedily as my age and good sense would allow.

I have been told that after visitations such as mine people are overwrought, that they sleep for days or meditate upon the wisdom they have been given. And this may be so—I cannot say that my experience is the common one. But what I felt as I walked was a cheerful normalcy, a return almost to my more carefree days before my troubles. There was someone willing to walk the way with me and forgive me, I thought, and that counted for much. The work that lay ahead seemed less onerous, the sorrows less complete. It was not so much that I had been helped to bear my burdens as that I had been reprieved from my self-doubt and self-recrimination. I may have whistled on my way to the hut; I know I sang from time to time.

When I returned I found Job sitting outside the hut in the morning sun, his head resting against the uneven boards. He was watching the desert, and when he saw me he smiled. I did not ask him how he had managed to leave the hut, and he did not ask why I was in the desert, but as I sat next to him he took my hand, and for a long time we sat together without a word.

At last Job said, "Hadasa, I have talked with a god who asked me questions."

I looked at him. His eyes were very bright as he watched the distant horizon. I squeezed his hand and said, "So have I."

The scribes would have you believe that after our visitation Job's fortunes reversed, but that is too easy a story—there was still much to do and much to suffer. But Job felt better from that moment, and continued to feel well. I had felt that the break in Job's fever had been a process of disease—he had plunged into great illness after short plateaus of health so often that it I barely noticed his days of recovery. But as days passed he remained alert but tired, and ate everything I brought him. And then he sat up by himself for days, and then he stood, and then he walked.

And then it was time to plant, and we had to travel to Shuhua to manage our lands, two aging workers in the lingering cold, with all the pain of bending and hard work in the hard earth. But Job could work and plan again, and he did small jobs for Calev and the judge and the others of Uz, and we did not have to beg again. And as it became clear that Job's illness had passed, we were able to return to our home; and though it was cleared of our possessions it cheered us to once again have our own.

Job had been right, and we did gain back a great deal with our next harvest—still more the next. Once again, it seemed that all that Job touched turned to his favor, and after the third year of our troubles we were as rich as we had ever been. Richer, even, for in the second year Behira had received word of our reversal of fortunes and in the third year she and Job had a little girl, whom they named Leah, for our sorrows.

But there were, and still are, those nights when any of the three of us may lie awake in tears for the family that we had, for the loved ones we had and which are lost. Job chides us, sometimes, for dwelling in the past, for not celebrating our fortunes. But it is God's blessing to mourn and remember, and Job calls his children to mind as much as we do. On nights when he and I lie together, we often talk of Naomi's wisdom, or Zafrir's energy, or any of our children who were, and we find no shame in mourning their absence.

Job has married again, three young girls—I suppose they are older than I was when I married Job. It is difficult not to resent them for their youth, their growing families. I still hold the keys of the household and the love of my husband, but his interest is taken often by his new children and his new fortunes. Thus the fire of God that burned Job and then renewed him still scatters its ashes in my life. But it is not a strange thing, something whispers to me from time to time, to resent the ones you love and yet to forgive them.

I am very old now and may soon die, and yet I can say that my end days are greater than they were before our sorrows. For, though my children have been taken from me, I know that God knew their names and that I can say what perhaps few can say, that he has wept with me for them. This, then, the measure of my life: that I may say without question that God knows of me and I of him. And therefore I end my story: I am Hadasa, wife of the merchant Job.

THE FINALE COMES SO BRIGHT / WE STOP SEEING, AWED . . .

Keep me as the apple of the eye, hide me under the shadow of thy wings . . .

The Aftermath of Explosion

The finale comes so bright
we stop seeing, awed
by the clap and thud,
by the thudding clap,
the thud that shakes
you past your shoes,
that shakes your shoulders
searching for your wings
for your wingblades.
I gave you my wings—
I gave you my wings to keep
until the finale ends.

. . . THE BEAUTY OF WINGS, / OF ANGEL WINGS . . .

And I said, Oh that I had wings like a dove! for then would I fly away, and be at rest.

I want the beauty of wings,
of angel wings angled
upward, angeled upward,
the curve and thrust to heaven,
overlapped, heavy, halcyon—
halcyon. . .
And then again, a
mute swan sleeping
head hidden
within the white.

IF YOU SEE ME SMILE AT THE FINE COMMOTION . . .

The preacher sought to find out acceptable words: and that which was written was upright, even words of truth.

Lingua Doctrinae

amicus, amici, amico, amicum, amico,
Amice.
The window, with its morning salty joke
of squinting scowls, unfolds a dusty yellow ray
of light on you, while I still close-eyed soak
in shadows in the middle of the room.
We resurrect the third declension, bring
the plural genitive alive, resume
linguistic worship, conjugate the Mass, and sing
our hallelujas, pater nosters, pronoun penance
for our poor grade in repentance
for our reprobate translation of this sentence.

deus, deo, deum, deo, dive,
Dei.
I sit below the window, left of center;
you sit arch and rightly right, and see
what all the rest of us believe, and whether
it is worthy, dull, grammatically lax,
or nonsense, and your hand leaps, choking,
when we have ill-grasped the graceful syntax
of salvation, and what have we all been smoking
that we think theology the ancient tongue
of piety, apology the young
and ransomed language of the Son?

intellego, intellegere, intellectum
Intelleximus.
If you see me smile at the fine commotion
of your indignant lexicon run loose,
it is only I am stirred by your devotion
in a faith not made a choate firstborn lamb
to the locution of our system. If I sometimes
wade too quickly into contradiction, dam
your vivid prosody before the rhyme
and reason have made art of argument,
and if my nettled morphological dissent
insists on rising, I am confident
that though your own religious phonotactics
may be the far side of the room from my intent,
the formal phonemes of my own ascent,
I doubt to disagree with the semantics
of your faith, and neither your celestial-bent pragmatics.

I TOUCH HER I KISS HER I LOVE HER . . .

And I went unto the prophetess; and she conceived, and bare a son. Then said the Lord to me, Call his name Maher-shalal-hash-baz. For before the child shall have knowledge to cry, My father, and my mother, the riches of Damascus and the spoil of Samaria shall be taken away before the king of Assyria.

Maher-shalal-hash-baz

When I come into my wife
I've more expressions of love
than loss
as we conceive your omen.

I touch her I kiss her I love her
she moans.
Then we, side by side, spent, consider
not the act not the seed not the womb not the child

but the ceiling
and the larksong
and the laughter of someone else's children
playing on the street.

HE NEVER TALKS ABOUT THE SUN IN JUNE, THE STATE OF THE WILDFLOWERS,
OR THE BEAUTIFUL BLUE OF THE SKY . . .

Do they provoke me to anger? saith the Lord: do they not provoke themselves to the confusion of their own faces? Therefore thus saith the Lord God; Behold, mine anger and my fury shall be poured out upon this place, upon man, and upon beast, and upon the trees of the field, and upon the fruit of the ground; and it shall burn, and shall not be quenched.

Jeremiah, à la Ogden Nash

If you've read the Bible once or more,
You know that Jeremiah's a bore.
He prattles on and on. He won't diminish:
His theme is such you do not even want to finish.
While other prophets like good old Solomon talk about their wives or the other good
    things they've gotten,
Jeremiah rattles on about the death of Judah and how wicked all men are and how things
    are generally rotten;
He never talks about the sun in June, the state of the wildflowers, or the beautiful blue of
    the sky,
he rather asks, "Why will ye die?"
A question (in any age) that's hard to answer:
One cannot simply say, "Because my time's run out" or "I've come down with a deadly
    pancreatic cancer."
And anyway, with Jeremiah's attitude, the question should rather be: "Why will ye live?"
Certainly, to that, not an answer will he give.
Everything is just bad, bad, bad, and for certain getting worse, as he foretells all the people
    dying and their corpses getting smellish,
for some reason he devolves on this with relish.
He mourns the severing of the roots of David with brio, like some semitic dryad;
it's not a wonder that according to the OED he forms the etymology for the modern word
    jeremiad.
He dwells upon his subject once, then twice, then even thricely,
Then says "Woe is me now!", which is putting the matter rather nicely.
Then, when finally he feels his work is done, and we're in a panic, or at least somewhat
    nervous with our various fears,
he stops and thunders to us that we all should put on a brave face and dry our tears,
and tells us that, of course, God will remove our tormenters, if we pray and if we're good—
in the case of Jeremiah, I wish God would.

. . . HE JUST SHRUGGED HIS SHOULDERS, DICTATED THEM TO BARUCH AGAIN . . .

Then the word of the Lord came to Jeremiah, after that the king had burned the roll . . . saying, Take thee again another roll, and write in it all the former words that were in the first . . .

How to Get Over It

A PUBLIC SERVICE MESSAGE

The Jeremiah Method.

Jeremiah spent a great deal of time in prison and on more than one occasion had people trying to kill him as well, which is bad enough to be sure. But once, King Jehoiakim took the prophecies which Jeremiah and his sidekick Baruch had carefully prepared for the king's benefit and "cut [them] with the penknife, and cast [them] into the fire that was on the hearth, until all the roll was consumed in the fire that was on the hearth."

Now, Jeremiah had not only spent a lot of time working on these prophecies, but really, he was doing that jerk Jehoiakim a favor. And on top of all that, these were *prophecies* he'd burnt up! Jeremiah had every right to be angry. But instead, he just shrugged his shoulders, dictated them to Baruch again, and "added . . . unto them many . . . words."

So the Jeremiah Method is this: Lose yourself in the work of the Lord. Which is actually good advice, come to think of it.

. . . THE VALLEY OF BONES AND ALL THAT $#!X.

So I prophesied as I was commanded: and as I prophesied, there was a noise, and behold a shaking, and the bones came together, bone to his bone. And when I beheld, lo, the sinews and the flesh came up upon them, and the skin covered them above: but there was no breath in them.

Them Bones Them Bones Gonna— Walk Around

(A BAR SONG)

Look, you know this Jesus stuff, right? You seen that Da Vinci movie? Ever read the Gospel of Thomas? That $#!X's hardcore, man.

Look, you know that song? Your grandma prob'ly sang it. Mine sure as #Σ££ did. Them bones them bones—the valley of bones and all that $#!X. You know what I'm talking about. So the prophet, see, the song says, what—help me out here—dadada connected them dry bones dadada the word of the Lord something something them bones them bones them Φ%¢*!Ħ' bones and they're walking around or something—Φ%¢*, I don't re-member. ‡@++!X. Anyway, the song acts like it was the prophet dude who made the stupid bones walk around. And that's &%££$#!X, man. Total &%££$#!X.

Look, you know how those Φ%¢*!Ħ' medieval monks took all kinds of $#!X out of the Bible like this bones $#!X? They totally cut out the best parts! Like where that prophet dude grabs a Φ%¢*!Ħ' spear and slams it up in the Φ%¢*!ĦØ skeleton's brains, man. I'm serious. He's like Hyah! with the spear over his head all horizontal-style and his other hand out in front of him like he's Φ%¢*!Ħ' Jet Li. That dude's &@‡@$$. Anyway, the prophet dude's all flippin' around and Φ%¢*!ĦØ up the skeleton's brains. It has to be the brains, dude, their Φ%¢*!Ħ' brains. Always the brains. Anyway, he like runs up rocks and swings the spear 'round and smashes their skulls to Φ%¢*!Ħ' #Σ££. Huge mess. Skeleton brains all over the place. Maybe a couple bloody eyeballs. You know, that kind of $#!X. But what's he gonna do? It's a whole valley of Φ%¢*!ĦØ skeletons! A whole Φ%¢*!Ħ' valley! There's nothing he can do! They're gonna Φ%¢*!ĦØ swarm him! You can't beat skeletons, dude. That's a fact. Not a Φ%¢*!ĦØ valley's worth, that's for sure. But still. That dude was Φ%¢*!Ħ' awesome. Total maestro of ninja-style brain damage. Φ%¢*!Ħ' awesome. But you won't find that $#!X that in the Bible. Those Φ%¢*!Ħ' medieval monks took all that $#!X out. I hate those dudes. Φ%¢*!ĦØ monks. That's why the Bible's so Φ%¢*!Ħ' boring.

Look, all I'm saying is how the #Σ££ are we supposed to know how to survive the Φ%¢*!ĦØ skeletons at the end of the Φ%¢*!ĦØ world if the ‡@+Ħ Bible doesn't tell us how to kill them anymore? God is awesome, man, but if the Φ%¢*!ĦØ Bible's lost the rules on killing skeletons we're all going to be toast, you know what I'm saying? #Σ££. Φ%¢*!ĦØ monks. What the #Σ££ were they thinking? We're good as dead, man. Φ%¢*!Ħ' #Σ££.

Buy you a beer?

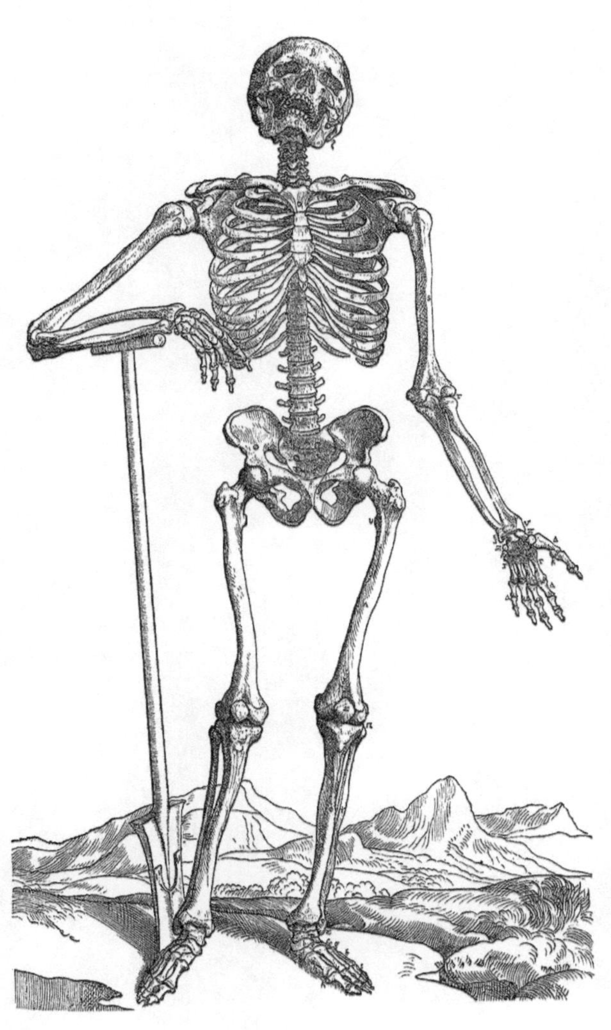

. . . MENE MENE TEKEL UPHARSIN

This is the interpretation of the thing: MENE; God hath numbered thy kingdom, and finished it. TEKEL; Thou art weighed in the balances, and art found wanting. PERES; Thy kingdom is divided, and given to the Medes and Persians.

From the Book of Daniel

It is not so much
that you are cradling your face
in your fists, your forearms
swelling out of split sleeves
like indecent thighs,

not so much
your cleft-chin grin,

nor even yet
your eyes as still as ice
on the pond, wrinkled at the corners
and shielded by twin sheets of Plexiglas—

but a single hoop of whitened gold
that scratches a holy fingernail
on the wall of my heart:

mene mene tekel upharsin

So, Daniel went in to the lions . . .

Then the presidents and princes sought to find occasion against Daniel concerning the kingdom; but they could find none occasion nor fault; forasmuch as he was faithful, neither was there any error or fault found in him.

𝕿𝖍𝖊 𝕯𝖆𝖓𝖌𝖊𝖗𝖘 𝖔𝖋 𝕴𝖉𝖔𝖑𝖆𝖙𝖗𝖞

The princes didn't like Daniel.
No, they didn't like him a lot.
That's why all his friends with the strange-sounding names
were thrown in the furnace, so hot.

They needed a way to destroy him.
They wanted something that would stick.
So they got the poor king to declare himself God.
They thought that just might do the trick.

Daniel, you see, was a good man.
It wasn't the king that he feared.
(He mostly just thought it was odd to be praying
to a man who had just permed his beard.)

So the princes accused him of treason.
They complained to the king—oh, and *how!*
So the king, having no better option,
decreed Daniel was now lion chow.

So, Daniel went in to the lions,
who hadn't been fed for a week.
That would have been curtains for Daniel
if an angel was not there to speak.

So, the story, it ended up happy.
To the lions the princes were threw—
but whom did they pray to when the den doors were closed?
I don't really know.
Do you?

HATRED IS ONE THING / THE USUAL THING.

And the Lord said to Hosea, Go, take unto thee a wife of whoredoms and children of whoredoms . . . So he went and took Gomer the daughter of Diblaim . . .

Gomer

He didn't know
growing up poor;
He'd never tasted death.

Hatred is one thing
the usual thing.

Prophesying is another.

Besides.
Husbands don't pay.

. . . GOD DID HIM ONE BETTER . . .

Now the Lord had prepared a great fish to swallow up Jonah.

Playing With Fire

When Jonah decided
to abort him his mission—
God did him one better:
put him big fish in.

"NO ONE MENTIONED THAT EVERYONE IN THE CITY,
STARTING WITH THE KING, WAS TOTALLY CRACKED."

Arise, go unto Nineveh, that great city, and preach unto it the preaching that I bid thee.

The Faith of the Ocean

Jonah's brother Abiezer got a pet herring for his seventh birthday. They named it Tiglathpilasser. His brother kept it in a pot on the floor between their sleeping mats and fed it grass, ants, horseradish, leaven, and, of course, dirt. Naturally, it committed suicide within a few weeks.

It was a rather shallow pot for a herring to live in but Tiglathpilasser was usually so undernourished that, from his fishy perspective, the possibility of jumping out barely existed. He resorted to that only when all the other methods by which a captive may traditionally resist its captors—political fasting, refusing to speak, occasionally playing dead—had failed.

Jonah was sleeping on his side, facing the herring pot, mouth open, drooling just a little. Tiglathpilasser, who had been shocked by the scorched, airless void in which he discovered himself, wriggled forward in relief upon discovering this open refuge of damp.

Jonah swallowed, awoke for an uncomfortable moment, squirmed over onto his other side, and was asleep again before he knew he had been awake. The muddy water in the vacant pot moved back and forth in silent, miniature waves. In the morning, Abiezer cried.

The herring lived for three more days. They never figured out what had happened to it.

Abiezer was brilliant. It was well known. He was forever in the back room, hunched over their father's Torah, muttering to himself. He fasted a lot, and was always having intense conversations with the scribes from Capharabis. The town elders of Meded-shobai loved him. The girls of Meded-shobai preferred Jonah.

Jonah was barely literate, but he

was a good-looking kid. This was what his father told the elders every time he did something wayward: "Well, he's no genius, but he's a good-looking kid." Jonah himself was fairly certain that there was something amiss in his father's logic, but generally didn't say so.

He was good at camel racing. Also stoning people. Not that he had ever actually stoned anything except a stray goat that he and Giloh, the son of a fishmonger across town, found wandering through the town square when he was fourteen. Gil had decided that it was probably an adulteress goat, and should be punished. They tied it up to a boulder behind Jonah's house; it keeled over with only a few good shots to the head.

"What was all that noise?" Abiezer asked when they came in after the goat was dead.

"We were stoning a goat," Gil said frankly.

Abiezer's eyes waxed very large. "You stoned a goat? What goat?"

"Just one we found." Jonah hung over Abiezer's shoulder and peered at the tiny characters. "Whatcha reading?"

"Do you know the punishment for slaying a goat not for food or sacrifice? Or for stealing a goat? Or for slaying your neighbor's goat? You'll be—"

"I suppose," Jonah said doubtfully, still staring at the scroll, "we

could go and bury it. What is this about locusts?"

Abiezer snapped the scroll closed and favored him with a disapproving expression. The adulteress goat subsequently became an Assyrian queen, and they gave her a sumptuous funeral, well outside of Mededshobai. Gil dug the hole and Jonah wrapped the poor beast in a sackcloth and pushed it in. They both beat their chests and wailed.

"Are you going to tell?" Jonah asked Abiezer that night as they lay in bed. His brother was itching to notify the authorities, Jonah knew.

"I don't know," Abiezer said stiffly.

He never did tell. Jonah concluded that this meant the fraternal consciousness in his heart just slightly outweighed his sensible knowledge of good and evil, and was a little nicer to him after.

Abiezer talked to God a lot. One day, God talked back.

"I'm going to Nineveh," Abiezer announced that night at dinner. It was a few years after the goat incident.

His mother dropped her spoon with a clatter. "You are not," she said.

Abiezer tried to look defiant. The effect was distasteful. Jonah thought he looked constipated. "Can I come too?" he asked.

"Nineveh is a city of sin, and the Assyrians have set at naught the will of the Lord," their mother continued calmly, ignoring her younger son. "What do you propose to do there?"

"Nineveh needs a prophet," said Abiezer very piously, "and I think it is to be I." Abiezer always spoke in very proper Hebrew.

"They'd kill you just for being Israelite."

"Then they can kill me." Abiezer's spoon, too tightly held, rattled a little against the table.

"I don't want to go to Nineveh, really," Jonah explained. "I want to go to Tarshish. The Frenklian-Kuhve International Camel Cup finals are being held there this year."

"They're not really in the same direction," their mother said. "When Nineveh grows up and stops whoring, Nineveh can have a prophet. And even then, who says it should be you? God?"

"Well," Abiezer said. "Well. I don't know. I mean—God? It wasn't *God*. It was—well. It was a significant . . . "

Their mother looked at him, waiting.

" . . . kind of a feeling," Abiezer finished at last, his voice sharp and low.

"Maybe you should be the prophet to Tarshish," Jonah suggested.

"You are not going to Nineveh," their mother said firmly, "until God sends your mother a significant feeling, too."

"All right," Abiezer said.

Jonah thought the ex-prophet looked a little relieved.

"*Go to Nineveh,*" said the voice in Jonah's head.

"Don't you mean Tarshish?" Jonah muttered sleepily. He had been dreaming about camel racing.

"*Nineveh,*" the voice repeated.

"Abiezer?" Jonah whispered. "Ab, no one's going to Nineveh. Do you want to go to—"

"*Abiezer who would have been my servant has denied my voice,*" the voice in his head told him. "*Go to Nineveh and call my children back to me.*"

"You have children in Nineveh?" Jonah said aloud.

"*My children in Nineveh will forever endure the torments of hell and the desolation of severance from their God, because they will not hear my voice.*"

Jonah sighed and forced himself into real consciousness. "I thought the children of Israel were your children."

"*I have many children.*"

"Yeah, many Israelite children."

"*Many children.*"

"There're twelve tribes of us!"

There was no response. Jonah groaned and struggled to his feet. "Okay," he said, pulling his ketonet over his head, "but you know, I've never even read the Torah. I mean, I know the parts that Abiezer quotes a lot, but—"

"*You will have my word and my voice. It will be enough.*"

"Yeah, but Abiezer knows all about abominations and plagues of locusts, too. Are you sure I wouldn't make a better prophet to Tarshish?"

The silence in his head as he finished dressing and slipped out of the house was deafening.

He arrived at the port at Joppa six days later. "You know," he said under his breath, "I don't really have the money for this." He had taken what little money he thought he could get away with from the spare honey jar in the storeroom, and had sold his shoes to a tired merchant outside of Gezer just to feed himself on the journey. He had nothing left to sell and resisted the idea of stealing, since he didn't want to go the way of the adulteress goat.

"Any suggestions?" he asked the blue sky above.

There was no response. He stood leaning against the railing on a platform raised up from the dock. Three large wooden vessels, one of which was to go up to the port of Nineveh in only two days, swayed on the water, dark and gold-rimmed in the late afternoon light. Passage on it would cost fifteen shekels, at least.

"Any time," Jonah said. "Any time at all. I'm just—ya know. Just waiting. On you. Yeah." His voice raised a little in volume. Two scribes walking near him squinted at him distastefully and adjusted their direction.

Half an hour later, his scowl had deepened considerably. A passing mother whispered to her children that *that* was what they would look like permanently if they didn't stop making faces at each other. The sun was setting and the dock was clearing. At last, Jonah straightened up and away from the rail. He charged off toward the town, torn between fury that God had picked him up from his nice warm bed and dropped him in Joppa without a shoe to stand on, so to speak; and shame that he, a second-rate prophet who had never read the Torah or stoned a real sinner, couldn't figure out what to do next. It was a little comforting that he couldn't imagine Abiezer doing any better, no matter how much Torah he had read.

"Bet on tomorrow's race?" a large man with a northish accent called out to him from a doorway near the road. He was leaning lazily against the frame, swinging a small leather bag that Jonah assumed to be heavy with coin.

Jonah snorted. "Bet what? My hair?"

The man shrugged. "Just asking. You're a good-looking kid."

"What race is it?"

"South Gaza Finals. The top three go to Frenklian-Kuhve in Tarshish."

Jonah could hardly contain himself. "Camel racing?"

"What else?" The man gave the bag a little toss and caught it in his other hand. "You follow camel sport?"

"Oh, I've been camel racing since I was old enough to do it," Jonah breathed. "Is it too late to enter?"

The man gave a short, harsh laugh. "You want to race? Zabeh the Midianite is racing tomorrow. He's won every race this side of Shechem for the last six years. Zalmuna of Midian is racing. Obil the Ishmaelite."

Jonah dismissed the names with a wave. "Obil's never even placed at Frenklian-Kuhve."

The Northerner shrugged. "You can put your name in at the west gate. But you'll never come near the Amalekites. Their camels are without number."

Jonah could beat any of the boys in Meded-shobai, on any camel. The girls he wasn't sure about, because he had seen some of them take their camels at a pretty good clip, but the elders said that the Torah forbade girls from camel racing. Fortunately, there would be no girls, Jew or Gentile, racing in Joppa.

He sat astride his borrowed camel uneasily, waiting for the start of the race. Zabah the Midianite was only two camels down from him, looking menacing. Obil, at the far end of the row, had fallen off once already, but seemed to be sitting his rather brittle mount more comfortably since his harnesser had kicked it.

"And—*L'khu!* They're off!"

His camel took to the course almost without him having to tell it to. Within seconds he was well ahead of everyone but Zabah, whose camel's nose stayed consistently near his camel's shoulder through the whole race, and the largest of the Amalekites, whom he could hear swearing a few feet behind him. Once it got started, the race was almost boring. He crossed the finish line in a storm of dust and camel sweat.

The cheers of the Joppa crowd and the continued profanity of the very large Amalekite were entirely drowned out by a placid line of thought which seemed, to him, almost smug. "*It is conceivable,*" the voice said, "*that my prophet has more than my word and my voice at his disposal.*"

"Jonah son of Amitai of Meded-shobai is twenty shekels richer!" the chief arbitrator bellowed to the crowd, "plus free passage on a ship leaving for Tarshish today!"

"Don't you think you've double-booked me?" Jonah growled under his breath.

He lingered at the dock, watching sailors and passengers boarding the Tarshish-bound ship and the third, headed for Zaraphath. Zabah the Midianite walked by and slapped him on the back. "Coming boy?" he called. "The ship leaves in twenty minutes. I'm looking forward to seeing you on the course in Tarshish."

"Right with you," Jonah said, leaping after him.

"*You are not going to Tarshish,*" came the response.

"You sound like my mother," Jonah said.

"Excuse me?" Zabah slowed down and turned to stare at Jonah.

"Oh—not you. I'm just—you know—talking."

Zabah looked uneasy. "Um . . . anyway . . . you raced well, young

one. I look forward to meeting you again in Tarshish."

"*You don't listen to your mother either.*"

"Look, it's not like Nineveh is *going* anywhere," Jonah hissed.

"Is everything all right?" Zabah asked.

"Oh yes, I'm just—you know—practicing. A speech."

"For what?" Zabah was staring. "I mean, you're really good and all, but—don't you think it's a little arrogant, maybe, having a victory speech ready? Already?"

"*I'm warning you.*"

"Oh, get *off,*" Jonah almost shouted.

"Okay," Zabah said. "Okay."

The first three days on the way to Tarshish were beautiful. The sun played in a sky ornamented with the most delicate of cirrus clouds, and the water was a fortune in blues, purples, and greens, shot with gold where the light tumbled into it. Zabah lounged on the starboard deck, in a chair which he had specially constructed to recline and fold back up, sipped olive wine, and composed chiastic poetry to his favorite harlot back in Midian. The Amalekite who had come in third sat in his cabin sulking because he had lost to a crazy Israelite. Jonah paced the deck, distracted, usually in the way of the ship's crew. Fortunately Zabah, with the very best of intentions, had inquired about a bit as to whether the Israelite camel champion might not be a bit insane, and so word was had around the ship that he was crazy.

When Jonah had said to get off, it appeared that the voice had taken him at his word, and stayed behind in Joppa. "I'm sorry," he growled into the silence. "Look, as soon as I get to Tarshish, I swear, I won't even race, I'll turn right back around, I'll *swim* to Nineveh if I have to." His head stayed quiet.

"I don't know," Zabah told the sailors. "I've heard some strange things about the interior of Judaea. But still, he's a phenomenal camel racer."

"I know, I didn't even win that race, *you* won that race, I'm sorry!"

"You're no better than Abiezer," a voice in his head told him, but it was only his own mind. He didn't know how he knew the difference. His own thoughts were oranger, somehow. The other thoughts came in darker, and blue.

"There may be something in the water there," Zabah had said. "But he's a good-looking kid."

"Damn nutty Israelites," the Amalekite said.

"I'll go to Nineveh right now, just give me a way!" Jonah shouted to the

ceiling of his cabin on the night of the third day, and promptly fell asleep.

The storm came up from nowhere. Zabah was nearly thrown off his chair by the wind and the Amalekite spilled ink on the angry epistle he was writing to the camel-racing commission. The ship rose high on a sudden swell of water. The rain came slamming down on deck like wheat dumped from a sack. Sailors swarmed and bounded from all corners to tie down the sails and bail water off the side. Zabah, in a hurried retreat below deck, chair in hand, heard them crying every man to his god, and went to find Jonah.

"Hey Jonah," he said. "Sleepy boy. Jonah!"

Jonah woke with a start. "What? I won't go to Tarshish!"

Zabah took his shoulder and shook him a little. "Is it your god you're always talking to?"

"What?"

"You talk all the time, to no one. Are you talking to your god?"

Jonah shook his head. "God doesn't talk back," he said sadly. "I didn't go to Nineveh."

Zabah took a step back. "Your god is angry with you?"

"My God has left me," Jonah said. "Or I left him."

"Well, I think he's back," Zabah said.

Jonah took in the violent tossing of the room for the first time.

"There's a storm?"

"You might say that."

A sailor burst into the room. "You!" He launched an accusing finger at Jonah. "Who are you?"

"Jonah son of Amittai," Jonah said. "I am a camel racer." He shook his head. "No, I am a Hebrew, and I fear the Hebrew God, who made the earth and the sea."

"You're fleeing the god that made the earth and sea," Zabah pointed out.

"You're fleeing your God? You're bringing us to destruction!" the sailor shouted. "We cast lots, and it fell on you! Come on deck, both of you." He wrapped a burly hand around Jonah's wrist, lest he try to resist.

"How could the lot fall on me if I wasn't there to draw one?"

The sailor shrugged. "That Amalekite camel racer stood in for you."

"Convenient," Jonah muttered.

"*My will may be done even through an unreliable man of Amalek,*" the voice said.

On deck, the sailors were busily heaving various barrels and chests overboard. The ship's captain saw them emerge and ran over to gram the arm that Jonah's first captor was holding. "What do we do?" he shouted against the wind.

"It seems the Hebrew god is angry," Zabah told him.

"So how do we calm him down?" The captain was staring around wildly. "I mean—what do you Israelites do, child sacrifice?"

"No!" Jonah snapped. "Eeeww. Strictly pure animals."

The sailor who had apprehended Jonah below deck had noticed the chair Zabah was still carrying. "This is going to have to do," he said, taking hold of it.

"Don't!" Jonah put a hand on the chair. "Throw me overboard."

"Right," the captain bellowed. "Yes, absolutely, let's throw the angry god's only present constituent overboard. That'll definitely make him feel better!"

"I'm serious," Jonah said. "Cast me into the sea. The tempest is for my sake. I disobeyed my God."

"Can you even swim?"

"No," Jonah admitted. The rain against his face was turning to hail.

"Then forget it. Row harder!" the captain shouted.

"We're not going anywhere," one of the sailors shouted back at the captain. "The wind is too much. We're—" His voice was muffled by the rising wind, which was punctuated by the deliberate snapping sound of the lesser mast cracking.

"God will not lay my innocent blood on you," Jonah shouted at the captain. "Throw me overboard!"

Zabah dropped his chair, lifted Jonah from behind, and hurled him into the ocean.

The captain was somewhere far to the north of shock. "How could you just—"

"I believed him?" Zabah said shyly.

Did I mention I couldn't swim? The orange voice in his head was howling as he sank, flailing, through the ocean. *I'm not going to Tarshish now. But what about all your precious Ninevite children? Do you love them more than me? What is Israel to you, anyway? We're easy. We always come back. You don't even have to work for us—send one Midianite army into Joppa, and we're lighting dead animals on fire in a matter of minutes. You tell me to go to Nineveh, and I get up and go to Nineveh! You stop talking to me and I jump into the ocean, and now I'm drowning for you, and maybe I got it wrong, but in the name of Moses, I tried!*

He was so alive with his righteous indignation that he didn't notice he wasn't in the water anymore. He was falling still, but he was grounded, tumbling down a soft, unpleasantly moist slope. A moment later he slid to a halt, and he realized he could breathe.

"You will be returned to the earth in three days time," the voice said.

Jonah sat very still, exhausted and breathing hard and trying to ignore the ungodly stench assailing his lungs. "You might have spoken up a little sooner," he whispered. "How in the name of all your dead prophets was I supposed to know what to do?"

"It's called faith," the voice said. *"Go to sleep."*

"Where am I?" Jonah asked when he awoke. The air was foul, so putrid that it was painful to breathe, and he was very cold.

"You're inside an ichthyosaur."

"I'm what?"

"A great fish has swallowed you."

"It stinks."

"It has lived sixty million years beyond its time in preparation for this event."

"And it stinks."

"So did your intestines, according to that herring."

"Excuse me?"

There was no answer. Jonah bit his lip to keep the bile down. "Sixty million years? You knew sixty million years ago that I was going to disobey you and go to Tarshish instead of Nineveh?" Still no answer. "How can you say it's my fault? You could have stopped me."

"You chose."

Jonah exhaled loudly. "Okay. Sure. Have it your way. I don't suppose you prepared a nice fire or a heavy coat for this event along with your fish? Maybe some flatbread and avocado paste?"

There was something in his head he could only think of as a blue smirk. *"You could have been on a nice warm boat. I told you to take the nice warm boat in Nineveh."*

"But you knew I wouldn't!"

"You chose."

Time didn't pass inside the fish. It didn't move. Time was a place, a soft, wet, horrible place, wrapped in the stench of ancient fish innards. Time was a trap, insidious, deceptive, and unreal. He felt that he was always on the verge of vomiting, which was made worse by the hunger consuming him from the inside out. It was impossible to lie, sit, or stand comfortably, as the cavernous stomach rolled and spun him with the ichthyosaur's movements through the ocean.

He was cranky. He tried not to be, because really he knew that God had saved him after he had disobeyed, done really no better than his spineless brother; but he was tired and hungry and irritated with himself for being stupid and irritated with God for being right. The voice, he discovered, rarely answered him when he wasn't polite. Unfortunately, talking to the voice was really the only thing he had to occupy himself, and the silence the voice left when it went away for too long was unbearable.

"How long have I been here?" he asked finally.

"Two days have passed. In one day more you will return to dry ground."

"Thank God."

"You're welcome."

Jonah snorted, refusing to believe in a god with a sense of humor. "What am I supposed to do in Nineveh once I'm there?"

"Bring my children back to me."

"You've mentioned that. How?"

"You have my word and my voice."

"You've mentioned that too." No response. Jonah took a deep breath. "I'm terrified, you know." It was not something he had admitted to himself up till this point. "They stone the prophets in Nineveh."

"You fear Nineveh more than me?"

"Oh, I'd say the two of you are running about neck-and-neck."

"It is not wrong to fear. But your hope must speak louder than your fear, and your faith must be greater even than your hope."

"Hope gets a lot louder when it's metal-plated."

"Nineveh will not be what you think. Do you believe in a God who would truly leave you alone?"

"I believe my God put me in a fish for three days to teach me a lesson."

"*Three days could be spent in harder places, and for greater purposes.*"

"What's that supposed to mean?"

"*The children of your children's children may live to know.*"

"Great," Jonah said. "I'll tell the Ninevites that. Maybe they'll just put me out with the lepers."

The experience of being belched out of an ichthyosaur was one Jonah found he had no way to describe, and wanted intensely to forget anyway. It was the smelliest five minutes of his life.

He lay on the sand of a warm beach, drenched in sunlight, enjoying the relatively stenchless air. The ichthyosaur lay in a similar position a few yards away, basking in the sun and the warmth, barely moving, a good ten feet away from the water's edge . . . It took him a moment to realize that it was dead.

"You didn't have to kill it," Jonah said, surprised by his own feeling for his digestive-tract captor of the last three days.

"*Arise,*" said the voice, heedless. "*Go to Nineveh, and speak there the words that I shall give unto you.*"

"I was just on my way," Jonah sighed. He trudged out of the water and pulled his ketonet back on. "What direction is it? How far inland am I going? How long is this going to take? What am I supposed to eat? I still don't have any shoes. You'd think they would have given the winner of the South Gaza Semi-Finals a new pair of shoes, since he couldn't accept their very kind invitation to go to Tarshish and become a celebrity. Seriously, though, what am I going to eat? Don't you usually just rain pita bread when the prophets ask for it? I've been inside a fish for three days. I'm hungry."

"*North and west.*"

"Don't you mean east?"

There was no answer.

The thing he was not prepared for was the sheer enormity of the city. He stood on a hill overlooking the east gate, and found that he could not find an end to the metropolis in any direction. It was like looking off the edge of one world and into another. Another world where they sinned a lot and blasphemed the Lord and stoned the prophets and probably ate beasts of undivided hooves, the pigs. He began to pick his way down the hill, more carefully than he needed to.

The east gate was crowded with merchants and harlots and travelers of a general nature, camels and chariots going in and out of the city, and he didn't expect to be given any particular notice. The tunic and ketonet he had set out in were filthy, and he looked and smelled not just like a beggar, but like a beggar who had bathed in ichthyoid digestive juices. He expected to be ignored entirely.

"Hoo boy," said the first harlot who saw him. She was draped in red, reclining languidly against a boulder near the road, watching the comers and goers and slinking lazily to her feet when the richer merchants noticed her. "Need a place to stay tonight?"

"I might," he said, "but I don't have any money, so I was thinking maybe I'd find a—barn or something that someone wasn't—"

"A barn?" she said. "In Nineveh?" Her smile was slow and delightfully lethargic. "Where do you come from?"

"Meded-shobai," he said.

"Never heard of it." She smirked and stretched her sinuous neck. "The second street from the square. Look for the Vintage House, west of the gate."

"Yes," he said. "I can stay there?"

"Ask for Rizpah." Her eyes slid from his face downward. "Don't worry," she whispered, "I won't make you pay."

He nodded. "Thank you," he said, and turned back toward the gate.

The flow of people entering was prodigious, and so well-mixed that he expected he would do all right remaining inconspicuous, fish-stained clothing and all.

"You!" a sharp voice summoned his attention. "Here." Jonah paused and turned toward the sentry, wondering if the smell on his clothes was more effective than he'd realized. "You have never been to Nineveh," the sentry told him. It was not a question.

"No," Jonah said. "Is it that obvious?"

"I know everyone who passes through this gate," the sentry told him. "And," he added in a more confidential tone, "you do seem a little hickish."

"Oh," Jonah said.

"But you're a good-looking kid," he continued. "Just get some new clothes and you might even find real work. Begging is not permitted in the upper district, or on the hill of my lord's house. My lord taxes seven percent of all proceeds, with a two percent increase per thousand shekels over four thousand shekels of income in the year. If you do not pay your taxes, my lord's guards will find you and quarter you. My lord's guards do not answer to beggars and will not protect you. If you need help, bribe someone. And stay south. If you die in the lower north district, no one will notice."

"Thank you," Jonah said uncertainly.

"Of course," the sentry added as Jonah was about to continue into the city, "you are not of Israel."

Jonah turned. He had neglected his Torah, but he had never denied his god.

"I didn't think so," the sentry said, rather as if he had through so, but wished to think otherwise. "I saw you speaking with that harlot. The men of Israel are usually more—private with their harlotry."

"What harlot?" Jonah said.

"And I've never seen a Jew so ill-clothed."

"These are nice clothes," Jonah objected. "I had a little trouble getting here is all."

The sentry shrugged. "All right," he said. "Just be careful. The Hebrews are not prospered in Nineveh." He hesitated. "You just seem a little—Israelitish." He was already turning his attention back to the road. "Something in your voice?"

Jonah stepped through the gate and found himself in a city full of people who wanted to stone him. "Now what?" he asked.

No answer. He walked forward.

There were two women watching him. They paced him exactly, a few feet to the left, but nearly perfectly parallel. They both stared shamelessly, their necks stretched forth to keep him in view. There was a tinkling as they walked. He realized after a moment they were wearing bells on their ankles. He had thought only lepers did that.

At first he thought it must be the fish smell. A lot of women stared at him as he went by, and the ones on the road with him adjusted their pace to stay near him. A few even switched direction to walk with him.

One young woman stood up from the yard where she was crushing grain and leapt into the road to seize his wrist and walk alongside him. "Hi," she said.

"Hi," he said.

"You're not from around here?" she said.

"Apparently not," he said. She was pretty, although she wore her hair uncovered and her robe swung above her ankles when she walked quickly, which made him uncomfortable.

"So what's your name?" she asked.

"Jonah son of Amittai," he said. "Can I help you?"

She tilted her head charmingly. "Do you have a wife?"

He pretended not to have turned and stared at her. "I don't."

"I think you're really cute."

"Oh," he said.

They walked on a few minutes in silence.

"Is that," Jonah said at last, "why all these women seem to be following me?"

The girl nodded, eyebrows drawn. "Yeah," she said hesitantly. "Or something."

"Are you hungry?" asked a woman selling stuffed eggplant and olive kebabs.

"I don't have any money, exactly," Jonah said.

The woman, who was middle-aged and looked as if she had probably borne several children already, seemed to melt at the sound of his voice. "Have a kebab," she breathed. She had bells on her ankles too.

He was just walking. He had been for hours. The city never ended, through it changed constantly, from market squares, to rich houses and chariots, to poor districts brimming with barefoot children. The parade of women behind him had attracted their own parade of men, boys who wanted to know what was happening, husbands following their wives and fathers their daughters, frequenters of the harlots who were just accustomed to following harlots, men who were simply intrigued by this migration of women. Jonah kept his eyes straight ahead, continued at a marked, rapid pace, and spoke to God the whole time. To his followers he was perfectly calm, self-possessed, and seemed to know where he was going; and for some reason, they were going there too. They were citizens of a city that knew only fear and pleasure, pain and wealth, death and lechery. They knew no god, but they found his evident calmness riveting. Jonah had never been so terrified in his life.

"It's not that I don't have faith," the orange voice was going on. "It's just that I don't really know how this is all going to work out, when I start preaching in the name of Israel's god, and they try to kill me, I don't see how that will really save any of their souls, and I'm just a little skeptical about you having kind of, you know, gotten off somewhere else for the moment. Okay, maybe I don't have faith. But it seems to me there's a time for testing a person's faith, and there's a time for sending down the lightning and tempests and all that. You were okay sending in the tempests to get me all repented up and ready to preach. I mean, I'm just saying. 'Cause there are getting to be an awful lot of them, and I think that actually it wouldn't take nearly this many to kill me straight up when they figure out about this whole Hebrew thing, so—"

"Here. Now. Speak."

Jonah halted so fast he stood swaying on one foot for several seconds before he regained his balance. "Okay. Okay. I'm all set. What do I say?"

The crowd of women slid to a halt behind him, and the men came sliding in behind them, and the two groups began to mingle, until at last there was no crowd of women and no crowd of men, but just one very large congregation of sinning Ninevites, waiting to see what this handsome young man from Judaea, who muttered to himself a lot, might do next.

Jonah turned slowly to face the Ninevites. They did not look angry. Nor, however, did they look repentant. They looked curious. They looked like they might try to kill him, but they also looked expectant, like they were waiting for instructions. Or for the starting gun, to launch the Hebrew-slaughtering fest.

"*Yet forty days*," he cried, "*and Nineveh shall be overthrown!*"

The silence that followed was prodigious.

"*That's it?*" he asked under his breath.

"*Yes.*"

Jonah's teeth began to grind just a little.

The crowd stood very still, swaying a little as will any human being standing on one spot for more than a moment, staring at him, and staring past him, and not seeming to really see anything. There was no sound. The air was warm and thick and light, and unsettled, as if something were hanging just above them all, something huge and prolix and fiercely blue. He could hardly keep his eyes on them. They were going to all start picking up stones at any minute.

Jonah turned around, teeth clenched, and kept walking. The crowd stayed behind. By the time they began to whisper, to speak, to cry their sins to the Lord and plead for his mercy, he was entirely lost, looking for the Vintage House. Even if Rizpah was a harlot, maybe she had a barn. He wasn't sure of how things worked with harlots, and if you could rent the barn without renting them, but Rizpah had been nice enough.

"*Only because you're such a good-looking kid,*" said a voice in his head, but he was too tired to decide what color it was.

He found Rizpah farther into the low district than the Vintage House was, surrounded by thin, barefoot children. She was sitting on the ground, distributing loaves of bread and honey candies.

"What on earth are you wearing?" he asked.

"I sold the garb of my harlotry to buy bread for the orphaned, and to dress in the manner of the Hebrew prophet," she said demurely, and turned her eyes up to him. Recognition flooded her face and she scrambled to her feet. "You!"

"You repented," Jonah said, incredulous.

"Yes," the harlot told him, not meeting his eyes.

"Why?"

"I heard the voice of God."

Jonah shook his head. "You heard *me,* Rizpah. Are you insane? You heard me. One sentence."

She just stared at him. "Weren't you there?"

He didn't really have an answer to that.

"I was looking for a place to sleep," he said after a moment. "I thought I might be able to stay with you."

"I don't *do* that any more, you Hebrew pig!" she yelped. "Get away!"

"No," he said, "no! For the love, I've been walking for about six days now, and I haven't eaten very much, and although I'm sure the fasting and self-abuse is making me extraordinarily holy, I'm just *tired,* all right?" She was staring, and he was fairly certain he was not behaving like a prophet. "Never mind." He turned and breathed. "I don't get this."

"Don't get what?"

"I'm not talking to you."

"Don't get what?"

"Not talking to *you,* either. Unless you have more threatening eight-word sentences you'd like me to wield against this sinful nation, I just want to go somewhere and sleep."

"I think that you could use a nap."

The sun was long set and most of the streets were not very well lit, but he found as he worked his way back toward the east gate that he was observing the most peculiar phenomenon. He was fitting in much better than he should have. Gone were the sumptuous clothes, the rich turbans, the ankle bells. Everyone he passed was dressed, as Rizpah had been, in the most ungainly, filthy, shapeless clothes he'd ever seen.

He found himself, as he drew nearer the edge of the city, walking alongside some nondescript, maybe-male-maybe-female sort of person. She was leading a cow wrapped in burlap.

"Why?" he asked as he drew alongside her, "is your cow wearing that?"

She turned to look at him, and he recognized the girl from earlier, who had thought he was cute. Her hair and face and hands were streaked with soot, as if she had been lying in the fireplace, and her robe was torn and dirty. And, he noticed, of a modest length.

"The manner of the Hebrew prophet," she whispered. "The humble riches of a man of God."

At last it dawned on him. "You're all—this is—how you think I dress?" He stopped walking and gazed down at his clothes. Some acid in the stomach of the fish had turned the brown wool of his tunic and ketonet thin and brittle, and faded the color to a dirty grayish. The tears and stains were exceptional. It looked like he was dressed in the stiff weave of sackcloth.

The girl turned her eyes up to his. "We are a repentant people."

"You're an unbalanced people," he said. "Who came up with this?"

"My lord the king," she whispered. "Who can tell if God will turn and repent, and turn away from his fierce anger, that we perish not? It is the law of the land."

"The king wasn't there to hear me today, was he?"

"No," she said, "but my lord sent out the decree the moment my lord's guard arrived at his house to tell him of the working of your miracles. My lord has ever been a wise king."

"One sentence!" Jonah shouted, throwing his arms out to either side. "This is not a miracle. This is eight words! This is not wisdom!"

The girl smiled. "You're cute when you're indignant," she said, and then, no more solemnly, "It's the will of the Hebrew God."

Jonah dropped his arms and strode away from the girl and her cow, furious. "I knew they were blasphemers here," he shouted, "No one mentioned that everyone in the city, starting with the king, was totally cracked."

"*At a certain point,*" said the voice mildly, "*you asked for a statute on unrepentant goats.*"

"Can goats sin? I don't really think goats can sin. I don't really know how they can be repenting."

"*They believe they are doing my will.*"

"And are they?"

"*Does it matter, so long as they believe? They are acting in the fear of God.*"

"They're acting deranged."

"*Why are you so angry? They are acting converted if, perhaps, undiscerning.*"

"And so they're all just forgiven now?"

"*Would that be so terrible?*"

"Well, I suppose I should have known. You're gracious. You're merciful. You're slow to anger. Sometimes. Not where it concerns large fish; you're pretty quick with the large fish. If only everyone could be so easily converted, with just the one ambiguous sentence, no one would ever need to stone a goat again. Or travel three days in a fish. Why am I even here? I could have gone to Tarshish. You could have sent anyone. You could have just written your sentence in the dirt. You could have plucked a good-looking kid from anywhere in Assyria."

The voice was definitely gone.

"I'm blaspheming!" Jonah shouted to the sky, "Why don't you kill me where I stand? Why can't I just die, now you've spoken your sentence through me?"

The east gate was closed. A sentry wearing what looked like raw camel skin stepped forward as he approached. "Gate closed at sunset," he said rotely. "No one in or out. Come back in forty days."

"It won't open tomorrow?" Jonah said.

"No one in or out," the sentry repeated. He sounded remarkably convinced, considering how little his voice changed pitch. "Nineveh is fasting and praying, that we perish not. We have but forty days to appease the Hebrew God. Who knows whether he will turn and repent?"

Jonah groaned. One of the other sentries moved forward and well-healed incisionspered something in the first sentry's ear. They both scrutinized him, and the first sentry leaned closer. "Are you him?" he asked.

Jonah sighed, "Yeah," he said. "I'm the guy with the fashion sense."

The other sentry reached forward and grasped Jonah's arm. "I knew," he said. "I knew, this morning, that you were Hebrew. I knew." He looked at the row of burlap-clad men behind him. "Let him out."

There was some uncomfortable shifting. "Order of my lord the king," one of them pointed out apologetically. "Forty days."

"Oh, get *off*," the sentry said. "My lord the king bows to the Hebrew prophet. Open the gate."

There was no shelter on the hill which he had come down that morning. He found some passable branches and used his ketonet to set up a two-sided shelter that would spare him the worst of the rising sun. He was asleep within moments. His dreams were terrible. In the morning, he pretended not to remember them.

He sat inside his half-shelter and gazed out at the city. Only a day before he had stood here and imagined it reduced to a smoking crater. Now they were all more righteous than he was, and were dressing like him to boot, and he was running away from God again.

A leafy shadow fell over his face, as if he were sitting under a tree, which he was not. He turned his head around slowly, uncertain what new ordeal to expect. There was an enormous, unreasonably thick vine hanging over him, growing straight up into the air and heavy with long, rounded, dark green fruit.

He stood up uncomfortably. The vine offered more shade than any vine should have, but then, it was ridiculous in a lot of ways. It was at least twenty feet tall, and braced by nothing. A fruit snapped off one of the lower trailers and tumbled to the earth next to him.

"Breakfast?" he said doubtfully.

He sat all day in the shadow of the vine, eating watery fruit innards and indulging in periodic indignation. Nothing remotely blue entered his head. He watched the city. No one entered or departed through the gate, and he could see very little movement inside. He could imagine a lot. Sometimes he imagined them all fasting and beating themselves and rolling in ashes. Sometimes he saw them returning to their sin, and the wrath of God blowing the whole place sky-high. He preferred the second vision. He was pretty sure it was not at all the case. Sometimes he talked to the plant. It was, right at the moment, his only friend.

The night was cool, but he pulled some of the lower leaves off the vine, which were very large, and slept under those. He awoke reluctantly before sunrise, to the sound of large wings flapping. He opened his eyes slowly and uncurled his wound-up limbs, indisposed to return to a world in which he was a bad prophet and God did things that made no sense. The sky was dismally colorless and the leaves had blown off of him and were scattered across the hill. He was colder than he had ever been inside the fish.

There was something large in the sky above him. He leaned his head back and squinted into the gray light. It was a great flying reptile. As he watched, it flew down just above him, bit off the vine a few feet above his head, and flew away with the top three-quarters of it in his mouth, trailing behind the worm and liberating large green fruit-missiles across the landscape. Jonah felt robbed.

"My—plant," he said helplessly. The beast disappeared into the distance. "You didn't have to kill it," he sighed, for the second time that week.

The sun was rising, and with it a bitter wind kicked up. Jonah pulled his legs up and wrapped his arms around them. "Are you going to kill me now?" he asked.

"*No,*" said God.

"You're killing everything else."

"*I don't often kill people.*"

"You killed my plant."

"*It was mine. Zucchini.*"

"Oh."

"*Slightly modified. A very sturdy stock.*"

"Yes. You do seem to go for the very large things. Fish and—"

"*Ichthyosaur.*"

"And—zucchini."

"*You don't pay attention to small things.*"

"I know," Jonah said quietly.

"*Why are you so angry?*"

He had missed several pages of the story, the part where the Ninevites spat upon him, and he cursed them in the name of the Lord, and they laughed and tried to stone him, and all they that mocked were struck by lightning or eaten by rabid she-bears or turned into rock formations, or *something,* so that everyone who stood near came to fear the Lord their God, and the miracles could be remembered forever in the nation of Israel, and Jonah could be praised for his courage and spirit of revelation. Somehow the unexamined rage of it seemed more justified without the admission of his broken expectation.

"I don't understand," Jonah said at last.

"*What don't you understand?*"

"The Ninevites. Why did they repent?"

"*Because they heard my word and my voice.*"

"One sentence," Jonah said.

"*Did you think so little of my word and my voice?*"

"It never works that way in Israel! Why them?" Jonah was gripping and tearing the dead zucchini leaves in his trembling hands, oblivious to the violence on the already-slaughtered plant. "*We're* supposed to be the chosen ones! We're supposed to be the—I don't know, the special ones, the inheritors, the first-born—why is it easier for the Ninevites? *Israel* is yours. Israel has strayed, and always come back, but here it's *Nineveh* that—" He groaned and flopped backwards onto the ground.

"*I bear different covenants with Israel and with Assyria.*"

"I know! We're your children. And they were all converted with one sentence. They found you like they find a cockroach in the meal. Barely had to have their eyes open." He crossed his arms over his eyes. "I was born a Hebrew, into a covenant with my God, and I have never read the Torah, and I—"

"*Jonah,*" the voice said, and the blueness in those two syllables was excruciating. "*Do you think that you don't know me?*"

A dead zucchini fell from the crumbling vine and rolled past his feet, down the slope and toward the city. Jonah sat up and watched it go. "You killed my zucchini plant," he said, uncertain whether he was being recalcitrant, and whether the voice would leave again.

"*Is that why you're angry?*"

"Yes." Jonah turned to give the zucchini plant a lukewarm kick. It leaned distinctly sideways and did not spring back up. "You might as well have killed me too."

"Was it your zucchini? Did you labor for it? Did you make it grow? It came up in a night, and perished in a night. What difference is it? Do you pity it?"

"You didn't have to kill it."

"As you pitied the ichthyosaur."

"Well, it stank, poor thing."

"I have pitied Nineveh."

He stood and gazed at the city, silent and rapturous in the morning light. "There was more sin here in a day than in all of Judaea in a year."

"They did not know me. They have repented."

"I know. They came to you. No lightning. No floods. No pillars of salt. Not a single stoning. No retribution at all. It is so easy for them, and they are not Israel. They are not your elder children. Why is it harder for Israel?"

"Do you think that you don't know me?" the voice asked again.

Jonah had no reply. The wind had died; the sun was hot and he missed the zucchini.

"I spoke to you in the night," the voice said, *"and you arose. Do you truly believe I could call anyone at all to be my prophet?"*

"I think anyone could have spoken eight words."

"Your brother reads from the Torah every day. He searches and believes that he prays, and every night he falls into sleep again having still failed to find me. He prays to a scroll, not to a
god. *He cannot find me in the words that he has not learned to believe. I spoke to him, and he could not tell whose voice it was that he heard, and so could be prevented from my will. Your brother could not do this for me."*

Jonah sank back into the ground, pulled his knees up, and wrapped his arms around them. "Abiezer does what he thinks is best," he said weakly. "He tries."

"But you, who have never read the Torah, could not be restrained," the voice went on, ignoring him. *"I told you to go to Joppa and you walked there barefoot. You disobeyed me once and so terrible was your desolation at having been abandoned of your God that you threw yourself into the storm and the sea, never believing that you would die."*

"I was terrified that I would die," Jonah objected.

The voice continued as if he had not spoken. *"You were afraid to approach Nineveh. You stepped through the gates of the city in dread, you opened your mouth to speak in fear, but never did you hesitate, and your hope was greater than your fear, and your faith was greater than the ocean. You never doubted your God, until he accomplished the thing that he promised: until his children were called back to him. Why do you doubt me now?"*

"I never had faith," Jonah said. "I never thought this would work."

"*Faith is a choice,*" God told him. "*You chose my will even when you did not understand it.*"

There was a very long silence.

"*Do you want a challenge?*" God asked.

"Certainly," Jonah said, "although not particularly if it involves travel by marine monster."

"*Arise,*" said the voice, "*and go forth to Judaea, and speak there the words that I shall give unto you.*"

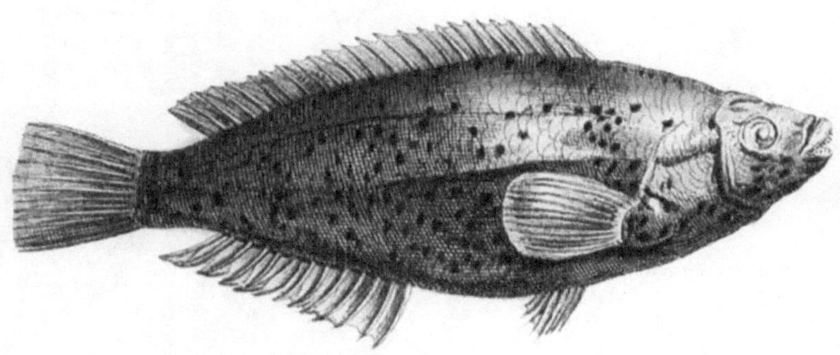

HE'LL ROIL WITH RINGING RHETORIC . . .

Woe to the bloody city! it is all full of lies and robbery . . . I will cast abominable filth upon thee, and make thee vile . . .

The Short Books

Now, Micah lives near Nahum
in the Bible's closing pages.
Micah is an optimist,
while Nahum speaks in rages.

Micah sometimes wishes
he lived near Lamentation.
It even could be better if
he moved to Revelation.

Habakkuk and Haggai
and Zephaniah, too,
have said that if he leaves them
they're going with him too.

So if someday you find the books
are all in disarray,
open up to Nahum;
Read the things he'll say.
He'll roil with ringing rhetoric,
he'll every point belabor.
And I think that I'm with Micah:

He'd make a very lousy neighbor.

"IF THAT'S WHAT IT TAKES, THEN SO BE IT."

. . . he shall turn the heart of the fathers to the children, and the heart of the children to their fathers, lest I come and smite the earth with a curse.

The Changing of the God

THUNDER! LIGHTNING!" Old Testament God raised his arms high and peered down at Earth through an opening in the dark storm clouds. "WHAT PART OF 'THOU SHALT HAVE NO OTHER GODS BEFORE ME' DO YOU NOT UNDERSTAND? DON'T MAKE ME COME DOWN THERE WITH ANOTHER PLAGUE!"

A beam of sunlight hit Oldie in the right eye and he turned, annoyed, to see the dark clouds parting, a white beacon clearing a path through the gray. A figure silhouetted by the light stepped forward. Songbirds and butterflies danced around this tall and lanky man while fluttering cherubs—chubby human-looking babies with the cutest little wings—scattered pink rose petals along his path. As the white-robed figure approached his features came into view: golden blond hair, sky blue eyes, and a smile that shone like a sunrise. It was, of course, New Testament God.

Oldie groaned. "YOU HERE TO KICK ME OUT?" His own two cherubim—four-legged creatures each with the faces of man, eagle, ox, and lion, and great brown wings—lay at his feet. One of them yawned.

"No way, Man." Newbie's laugh rang as a choir of children's voices. "I'm here to *love* You out."

"CUTE," Oldie said with a snort. He pulled at the tufts of wooly gray beard on his chin. "YOU'RE EARLY."

Newbie glanced down toward the Earth. "You ask Me, I'm long over-due."

"YOU THINK YOU CAN DO ANY BETTER? BE MY GUEST. THEY'RE A ROWDY BUNCH OF THIEVES, MURDERERS, ADULTERERS, AND BLASPHEMERS, EVERY ONE OF THEM. AND DON'T EVEN GET ME STARTED ON THE GENTILES!"

"No way, Man, don't be so hard on them! There've been some good ones."

"NOT IN YEARS." Oldie stomped up the clouds to his throne, a grand thing of gold and silver, lined with the finest diamonds and rubies. His cherubim followed close behind, the lazy flapping of their great wings causing windstorms in Africa.

"What about that Ezra fellow? Nehemiah? Malachi?"

"DEAD FOR NEARLY FOUR HUN-DRED YEARS NOW, IN PARADISE ALONG WITH THE CITY OF ENOCH AND THE FOURTEEN OTHER PEOPLE WHO'VE MADE IT IN."

"Whoa, Dude," Newbie said. He whistled in disbelief and the air around him filled with tinkling bells and minty freshness. "Are You serious?"

Oldie raised a wooly gray eyebrow.

"Oh, right," said Newbie. "Serious is Your shtick. Well We have totally got to do something about that skimpy Celestial population. That is like, the worst retention rate ever."

Oldie's fat lips curled into a smirk. "BELIEVE ME, I'VE TRIED EVERY-THING. I LAID THE LAW OUT FOR THEM TITTLE BY TITTLE, I GAVE THEM A LAND FLOWING WITH MILK AND HONEY, I EVEN HELPED THEM KILL THEIR ENEMIES, FOR MY SAKE! THERE'S NOT MUCH ELSE TO DO, UNLESS YOU GO WITH *HIS* PLAN." He pointed downward with a stubby thumb.

"Oh no, no," said Newbie, waving his perfectly-manicured hands in front of him, "not *that*. I was thinking of just the opposite, in fact. See, You've overburdened them with all these *rules*. Who needs rules? I'm thinking in order to get into *My* Heaven, you really only need one rule:" He made *Ls* with his thumbs and forefingers and framed an imaginary word in the air. "Love."

Oldie tapped his calloused fingers on his lap. "LOVE."

"Love. Like, whereas You're all like, 'Thou shalt love thy neighbor and hate thine enemy,'" Newbie said, imitating Oldie's thunderous voice, "I'm like, 'Dude, love *everyone*.'"

"EVERYONE."

"Yeah, everyone! Mind-blowing, isn't it? See, and You're all, 'Thou shalt not commit adultery,' and I'm like, 'Pshaw! If you're lusting after a woman, you've totally already com-mitted adultery in your heart.' And it's way not good enough to just not kill, 'cause if you're angry with your brother, you're *so* already in danger of judgment."

"WAIT," said Oldie, frowning. "I THOUGHT YOU SAID THERE WERE TOO MANY RULES. IT SOUNDS LIKE YOU'RE MAKING *MORE* RULES, NOT LESS."

"Fewer." Newbie smiled sheep-ishly. "You mean to say *fewer*."

Oldie sighed. "EXACTLY."

"No, You just don't get it." Newbie stretched his arms toward the sky and his cherubs flew up, throwing rose petals about like confetti. Trumpets sounded somewhere in the distance. "It's not about the *letter* of the law, it's about the *spirit* of the law."

Oldie shook his head. "THEY WON'T LIKE THIS. THE CHILDREN OF ISRAEL COMPLICATE THINGS ENOUGH ON THEIR OWN; THEY DON'T NEED THEIR GOD SPEAKING TO THEM IN RIDDLES. THEY LIKE THEIR BREAD FLAT, THEIR MEN CIRCUMCISED, AND THEIR LAW STRAIGHTFORWARD. NO FRILLS FOR ISRAEL."

"And that's another thing. I've been thinking, didn't We create *all* the peoples of the Earth? So in a way, aren't they *all* Our children? Why limit Our interaction with the children of men to just a small portion and condemn the rest to endless damnation? I'm thinking of expanding, going international."

An earthquake shook the Arabian peninsula and thunder echoed in the Grand Canyon as Oldie guffawed. "HA HA HA HA HA! DON'T SPREAD YOURSELF THIN, BOY. I'M TELLING YOU, IT'S HARD ENOUGH TO KEEP TRACK OF JUST THE TWELVE TRIBES. THE GENTILES HAVE THEIR OWN PAGAN GODS—LET JUPITER AND ODIN WORRY ABOUT THEIR WORSHIPPERS' ETERNAL SALVATION."

Newbie frowned, his light whiskers bristling in the folds of his furrowed chin. "Man, You used to be cool. When'd You get so darn cynical?"

Oldie peered at him from under half-closed eyelids. "TALK TO ME IN FOUR THOUSAND YEARS."

"Right." Newbie rolled his eyes and cleared away a section of clouds with a flick of the wrist. "Well, I'm going to get to work here. You're welcome to pack up and leave whenever You're ready."

"OH, NO," said Oldie. He was beaming now, in a brighter mood than he'd been in centuries. "I'M NOT GOING ANYWHERE. I HAVE NO INTENTION OF MISSING *THIS* SHOW." He slumped back in his chair and let out a great bellowing yawn. "BESIDES, THE JEWS WILL STILL WANT ME AROUND. THEY'LL NEVER ACCEPT YOU."

"Isn't that the problem? That they don't accept *You?*"

"OH, THEY ACCEPT ME. IN THEIR WAY. THEY'RE JUST CHILDREN, THOUGH. THEY NEED A GOOD SPANKING, NOW AND AGAIN."

The light of Newbie's complexion reflected in his cherubs' sparkling eyes. "I don't believe in corporal punishment," he said. "I believe in love."

"SERIOUSLY," said Oldie, exhaling through his majestic nostrils, "DON'T. THEY'LL CRUCIFY YOU."

"If that's what it takes, then so be it."

"Please, Son, don't."

"Oh, so now You're all chummy?" Newbie brushed away the butterflies and songbirds fluttering in his face. "Maybe You think the children of men are a lost cause, but I don't. So, *Father*, unless You're going to spank Me too—"

"Look." Oldie's nostrils flared wildly now, and he gripped the armrests of his throne. His fingers pressed into the gold. "I'm not being a pessimist. I *know* these people. They're not ready for You. They don't want some long-haired Teacher telling them to love each other. They want a Messiah, a general to lead them into battle. They want a wrathful God to destroy their enemies. And I'm not just talking about the Jews now. I'm talking about humanity."

Newbie tried to snort, but it came out more as a chorus of harps. "Aren't You the One Who's always saying they're just children? It's not about what they want, it's about what they need. They need love. *Real* love. Pure love."

"I'm telling You, they aren't ready. Wait about two thousand years, for example, and there'll be a generation of people who would wholeheartedly accept Your message of love and peace. Given the right circumstances, they could change the world with what You have to say."

"Good. They'll have My Word passed down to them from their ancestors."

Oldie shook his head. "By that point Your message will be so tainted by centuries of war and bloodshed in Your name, they won't want anything to do with You."

"War and bloodshed? In My name? *Hellooo*! Mems how *I'm* the One teaching them to love their enemy? It's *You* Who goes around promising inhabited lands to Your people, then commanding them to slaughter the current inhabitants. Don't worry about Me; no one will be killed in My name."

Oldie rested his chin on his knuckles, closed his eyes, and let out a sigh heavy enough to shake the heavens. His cherubim lay at the foot of his throne, snoring peacefully.

THE END.

ΑΝΑΓΚΗ

 Contributors

ARWEN TAYLOR

“Capitulation: Forbidden Squirming” [27]
“*Lingua Doctrinae*” [199]
“The Faith of the Ocean” [221]

Taylor is the author of one unpublished novel, half an unpublished dictionary, and a lot of unpublished conference papers.

B.G. CHRISTENSEN

“Abraham’s Purgatory” [45]
*The Official History of the Society for the Spiritual Attunement
of the Friends of G. C. Benefield*, Chapter 34 [79]
“The Changing of the God” [247]

Christensen, having successfully remade the Bible in his name, has as his next project a five-book series chronicling the final years of the superhero cult named after him, the Friends of Ben. He hopes this doesn’t make him sound egotistical.

DANNY NELSON

"Creation" [3]
"Under the Fifth Rib" [9]
"Original Sin" [13]
"Blood-Red Fruit" [15]
"Genesis" [25]
"Sustain-Able" [33]
"On the Ark" [35]
"Out of Heaven" [39]
"The Sacrifice of Abram" [51]
"The Excommunicate" [55]
"Isaac and Esau" [59]
"Jacob, to Esau" [63]
"A Travel Agent's Description of Egypt, Circa Moses" [67]
"Nailed" [97]
"Swinging" [99]
"Delilah" [105]
"Philistina" [109]
"Solomon's Lament" [113]
"From the Desk of Baal's Secretary" [129]
"The Queen Jew" [159]
"The Love Song of Eliphaz, Bildad, and Zophar" [161]
"The Book of Job's Wife" [163]
"Jeremiah, à la Ogden Nash" [205]
"From the Book of Daniel" [213]
"The Dangers of Idolatry" [215]
"Playing with Fire" [219]
"The Short Books" [245]

Nelson has been described by those who know him well as a mix of Dickens, Housman, and Woolf, and would be flattered if those friends had not been referring to his face. He has been known to read P.G. Wodehouse and E.M. Forster in the tub—simultaneously—and is not above mixing in his own stanzas when he quotes Dorothy Parker. He was born under the sign of the lion in the year of the monkey, and adherents typify his belly as cuddly and bear-like. He is the author of innumerable unpublished short stories, poems, and plays, and invents a neologism every month.

ERIC W JEPSON

"Blood-Red Fruit" [15]
"How Long Till Two Times" [29]
"How to Get Over It" [65, 107, 123, 125, 207]
"Solomon's Reprise" [115]
"Ezra's Inbox" [131]

Jepson (the W is silent) lives in El Cerrito, California, with his wife and their children and tens of thousands of earthworms. His first fiction-for-money was the short story "Afterlife"; since then he has made literally dozens of dollars in the field of literature creation. He also makes money teaching about literature created by other people.

GUSTAVE DORÉ
(1832 – 1883)

Illustrations

Doré loved his mother.

RYAN MCILVAIN

"Genesis" [7]

McIlvain is about half as cool as Sarah Jenkins. Pretty much everybody agrees with this, even Ryan. When he's not writing about himself in the third person, Ryan studies fiction in the MFA program at Rutgers University, Newark. His work has appeared or is forthcoming in *The Paris Review*, *The Potomac Review*, *The Chattahoochee Review*, *Dialogue*, *Irreantum*, and other magazines. He will begin a two-year Stegner Fellowship in fiction at Stanford University in Fall 2009.

SAMANTHA LARSEN HASTINGS

"Song of Deborah" [95]

Hastings is a librarian who likes to read, write, travel, and eat exotic foods.

SARAH E. JENKINS

"I Study Barnett Newman's *Adam* (1951)" [5]
"Weary" [61]
"Of the Blessed Dead" [111]
"The Palms of Her Hands" [127]
"The Aftermath of Explosion" [195]
"Wings" [197]

Jenkins recently completed an MA at Brigham Young University with an emphasis in contemporary American poetry (yes, she made it up, and yes, she got away with it). Sarah now plans to write contemporary American poetry at Northwestern University's MFA program.

THERIC JEPSON

"Along with the Rainbow" [37]
"Balaam's Sin" [71]
"Them Bones Them Bones Gonna—Walk Around" [209]
"Maher-shalal-hash-baz" [203]
"Gomer" [217]

Jepson is, allegedly, the same person as Eric W Jepson (allegedly). More details at thmazing.com.

WILLIAM C. BISHOP

"When I Do Go on My Honeymoon" [11]
"Moses und Aron" [69]

Bishop was born and raised in Boise, Idaho. After a two-year stint as an LDS missionary in Spain's Canary Islands he earned both a Bachelor's and Master's degree in Humanities from Brigham Young University. He currently lives in Lawrence, Kansas, where he is working towards a PhD in American Studies from the University of Kansas. Will is particularly proud of his status and reputation as a poetaster—that is, a shoddy poet.

The bulk of this book is set in **Galliard**, adapted by Matthew Carter for International Typeface Corporation (ITC) from type designed by the sixteenth-century master Robert Granjon whose work is often described as spirited or even spunky. Not bad for a 420-year-old corpse.

Title page, imprint, headers, and footers—the no-nonsense text—is performed by **Escrow-Roman**, designed by Cyrus Highsmith under commission from the Wall Street Journal, a no-nonsense newspaper. The Journal, like this Bible, uses engravery-style illustrations, although theirs, alas, were not crafted by Gustave Doré. Which is a shame, because it would be fun for old guys like Alan Greenspan to lounge around, telling their friends about the time they sat for Doré.

"Ezra's Inbox" is set in **Calibri**, a modern font designed by Lucas de Groot for Microsoft. Although a new font, as the default font in Word, Excel, Powerpoint and Outlook, Calibri is well on its way to becoming one of the most visible typefaces in the world. In addition to showing up in emails worldwide, Calibri, unlike former Microsoft defaults, has been popular among typophiles as well, winning an award from the Type Directors Club.

The dingbat used to separate the emails within that story comes from **Davy's Dingbats**, designed by David Rakowski, who is much more widely recognized as a composer of music. Designing fonts was something he did in the Nineties (until he grew out of it). Most of his fonts are adaptations made from scans, so the ultimate provenance of these swirls likely goes back much further than Rakowski's wild, bacchanalian, font-designing youth.

Fancy Text—a startlingly good match to the display font used in many period Doré books—was designed in 2003 by Claude Pelletier. Whether you call it gothic or blackletter, this austere font stands at the front of this Bible wearing a deep frown and voluminous satisfaction.

"Balaam's Sin" is set in **Courier New**—"the typewriter font." After Courier was designed by Howard "Bud" Kettler in 1955 for IBM's typewriters, the font was quickly appropriated by the industry. Courier New was introduced in the early 1990s as part of Microsoft's Windows 3.1 package and has become the standard for screenplays and overserious closet dramas.